GBBHunter

Logic

Elementary
Formal Logic

A PROGRAMMED COURSE

Elementary
Formal Logic

A PROGRAMMED COURSE

C. L. Hamblin

Professor of Philosophy,
University of New South Wales

METHUEN & CO LTD
11 New Fetter Lane London EC4

First published 1966 by Hicks, Smith & Sons Pty Ltd
Reprinted with minor corrections 1967.
(C) 1966 C.L. Hamblin
First published by Methuen & Co Ltd 1967
Printed in Great Britain by
Lowe & Brydone (Printers) Ltd, London

Distributed in the U.S.A.
by Barnes & Noble Inc

TABLE OF CONTENTS

Part 1

Logical Relations

Part 2

The Logic of Unanalysed Statements

Part 3

The Logic of Predicates

(Except as shown, starred chapters are optional additions to the course and may be omitted or taken later out of sequence.)

INTRODUCTION

This is a programmed course of the "linear" type, intended for students without previous knowledge of Logic, in early university years or in senior school. It is intended to supplement, rather than replace, lectures or classroom teaching: in universities it will lighten the tutorial load. It may also, however, be used as a self-tutor in conjunction with a text-book of a more orthodox kind.

The course is essentially elementary and does not lay claim to any special novelty of treatment. A possibly unusual feature, however, is emphasis placed on the seven classical "logical relations". The study of this ancient piece of doctrine provides an elementary trouble-free introduction to the concept of logical rigour, and the distinctions involved are basic to classical and modern logic alike.

An attempt has been made to break the course down into "more essential" and "less essential" parts to permit flexibility in the choice of topics. Broadly, those chapters that are starred in the Table of Contents can be omitted or taken later out of sequence.

The course represents from eight to 20 hours' work, depending on the student's speed of work and on whether optional chapters are included. Revision chapters are provided for the main parts of the course and are intended to refresh knowledge after a lapse of time.

HOW TO USE THE BOOK

The text of this book is set out in question-and-answer form. The answer to each question is underneath it, separated from it by a black line.

Start by covering all but the first question-frame with a piece of thick paper or card. Read and answer questions one at a time. Move the paper or card down to check your answer and uncover the next question.

You are urged to write your answers down on a separate piece of paper before checking them. This helps to ensure that you really make your mind up about each question before looking at the answer in the book.

The questions are supposed to be easy to answer so that you are carried along steadily by small steps. You will probably not give many wrong answers. When you give a wrong answer make sure you understand your mistake. If you find yourself giving more than a few wrong answers, go back and see if you can pick up some lost thread.

The course is divided into chapters, each designed to be completed at a sitting. Work at your own pace. You may do more than one chapter at a sitting, but it is better to avoid starting or finishing with a broken chapter.

Part 1
Logical Relations

Chapter 1: Statements and Logical Strictness

This chapter introduces the fundamental notion of a <u>statement</u> as something that may be <u>true</u> or <u>false</u>, and shows how logicians use the word "implies".

1.   When people use language -- that is, when they speak, or write using meaningful sequences of words -- they may make <u>statements</u>, or they may ask <u>questions</u>, or they may give <u>orders</u> or make <u>requests</u>, or various other things.

> "Cairo is in Egypt" is a <u>statement</u>.
> "How many fingers am I holding up?" is a <u>question</u>.
> "Please shut the door" is a <u>request</u>.
> "Canberra is the capital of Australia" is a ....

---

statement.

2.   "Who killed Cock Robin?" is a ....

---

question.

3.   "Please pass the salt" is a ....

---

request.

4.   Statements differ from questions and other forms of language in that they can be <u>true</u> or <u>false</u>. The statement "Australia is in the Southern Hemisphere" is ....

---

true.

5.   An answer to a question can be true or false but a question itself ...... be true or false.

---

cannot

6.   The statement "England is in the Southern Hemisphere" is .....

---

false.

7.   We do not always know whether a statement is true or false, but we always know that it is <u>either</u> true <u>or</u> false.
On the other hand, a question is .... true ... false.

---

neither .. nor

8.   (Read carefully)
It is not necessarily the business of Logic to tell us the <u>truth</u> or <u>falsity</u> of a statement. To tell us the truth or falsity of the statement "England is in the Southern Hemisphere" is the business of Geography, not Logic. In other cases the truth or falsity of a statement may be a matter of Arithmetic, Chemistry or Economics, or a matter of common knowledge, or experience. For example, the truth or falsity of the statement

"Zinc dissolves in Hydrochloric acid"
is a matter of ....

Chemistry.

9.   The business of Logic is to study the general properties of statements in so far as they may be involved in reasoning or inference. One such property of statements is the property of being true or false. Consequently the truth or falsity of the statement

"Statements are either true or false"
is a matter of .....

Logic.

10

10. The truth or falsity of the statement
                    "Two plus three equals seven"
is a matter of . . . .

Arithmetic.

11. The truth or falsity of the statement
                    "Questions cannot be true or false"
is a matter of . . . . .

Logic.

12. An important <u>logical</u> feature of statements is that the truth or falsity of one statement may depend on the truth or falsity of another. In particular, sometimes one statement <u>implies</u> another, that is, knowing that the first is true may enable you to deduce that the second is . . . .

---

true.

13. One statement S <u>implies</u> another statement T when knowing the truth of S would enable you to deduce or infer the . . . . . of T.

---

truth

14. Whether one statement <u>implies</u> another, in the logically strict sense of the word, is the business of . . . . .

Logic.

15. When we say "S implies T", using the word in its logically strict sense, the letters "S" and "T" represent . . . .

---

statements.

16.   When we say "Thunder implies lightning", since "thunder" and "lightning" are <u>not</u> statements, the word "implies" is being used in a logically (strict, non-strict) sense. (Which?)

---

non-strict

17.   We shall generally use the word "implies" in a logically strict sense. The same applies to the word "implication". Two statements S and T stand in a relation of implication when one implies the other. In this case the (truth, falsity) of one enables us to deduce the truth of the other. (Which?)

---

truth

18.   There are various other ways of expressing the relation of implication.   We can say that T <u>follows from</u> S, or that T <u>is a consequence of</u> S. If T follows from S then S .... T.

---

implies

19.   The statement "Six students attend this seminar" (implies, follows from) the statement "An even number of students attends this seminar". (Which?)

---

implies

20.   The statement "All Australian bears are mammals" (implies, is a consequence of) the statement "All bears are mammals". (Which)?

---

is a consequence of

21.   In ordinary speech we often indicate, rightly or wrongly, a relation of implication between two statements by using one of the words "therefore", "so", "consequently" or "because". If I say "Jones is middle-aged, so he's probably bald" I show that I think,

rightly or wrongly, that the statement "Jones is middle-aged" . . . .
the statement "Jones is probably bald".

---

implies

22. When someone says "S, because T" he shows that he thinks . .
implies . .

T . . . S
(in that order)

23. (Read carefully)
In ordinary speech, however, we do not usually use the word "implies",
or the other words referred to, as strictly as the logician does.
When the logician says that S implies T, he means that you can
deduce T from S without taking anything else for granted.
For example, consider the statements
    S: "This metal is platinum", and
    T: "This metal is valuable".

Here S implies T only If it is taken for granted that platinum is
valuable. Consequently, in the logician's sense, S does not imply T.

If someone says that "John Smith is a philosopher" implies "John
Smith is clever", he is taking for granted that . . . .

---

all philosophers are clever.

24. Even if it is true that all philosophers are clever (never mind
whether it is or not!) does "John Smith is a philosopher" imply "John
Smith is clever" in the strict sense?

No.

25. In our ordinary speech we (should, need not) try to use words
like "implies" in their strict logical sense.

---

need not

13

26. For one statement to imply another it is not necessary that either statement be actually true. All that is necessary is that the statements should be related so that if the first one is true the second is . . . .

---

true.

27. "T can follow from S independently of whether S is actually true." True/False?

True.

28. Whether statements are actually true or false (is, is not necessarily) a matter of Logic.

---

is not necessarily

29. If someone says that "Canberra is in Australia" implies "Canberra is in the Southern Hemisphere.", what statement is he taking for granted?

"Australia is in the Southern Hemisphere".

30. Is it true in the strict logical sense that "Canberra is in Australia" implies "Canberra is in the Southern Hemisphere"?

No.

31. Consider the statements:
      S: "Australia has full employment", and
      T: "Australia suffers from inflation".
Full employment may or may not cause inflation. In order to know whether S logically implies T, do you have to know whether full employment does cause inflation?

No.

32.   In future, when we use the word "imply", we shall normally mean it in the strict logical sense.   In this sense, <u>does</u> S imply T (in the previous example)?

No.

33.   (Read carefully)
However, even in examples in Logic books, it would be intolerable to insist on too many fine and subtle verbal points, and a certain amount of commonsense latitude must be allowed.   For example, we might raise no objection to saying that "Smith is a bachelor" implies "Smith is unmarried".   We would say, that is, that "bachelor" simply <u>means</u> "unmarried man", and that the assumption "All bachelors are unmarried" is, consequently not a factual assumption at all.

For the logician, as for everyone else, life is too short for unnecessary quibbles and legalistic points.   Logicians sometimes, no doubt, overdo things; but generally, when the student thinks unnecessary distinctions are being made, he would do well to ask himself if he has not missed some point of importance.
And conversely, when the student is tempted to indulge in hair-splitting, he should ask himself whether it is worth it.

Does "Jones is an uncle" imply "Jones is male"?

Yes.

34.   Does "Sydney is south of the Equator" imply "The Equator is north of Sydney"?

Yes.

35.   However, does "Copper is a metal" by itself imply "Copper conducts electricity"?

No.

36. To deduce "Sydney is in Australia" from "Sydney is in New South Wales", do we need the additional assumption "New South Wales is in Australia", or not?

Yes.

37. To deduce "Sydney is in Australia" from "Sydney is in New South Wales and New South Wales is in Australia" do we need the additional assumption "When one thing is in another and the other is in a third, the first is in the third", or not?

No. (This would be splitting hairs).

38. "In Logic, as in other subjects, we make distinctions not for their own sake but only when we think they are important."
True/False?

True.

END OF CHAPTER 1

Chapter 2: Implication and Equivalence

This chapter introduces and defines the logical relations "super-implication", "subimplication" and "equivalence", the first three of the traditional seven logical relations.

1.   "The characteristic of statements that distinguishes them from other forms of words is that they are true or false." True/False?

True.

2.   "The truth or falsity of one statement may sometimes be related to the truth or falsity of another statement." True/False?

True.

3.   When two statements S and T are so related that if S is true T must be true too, S is said to ..... T.

---

imply

4.   When we use the word "imply" in its correct logical sense, "S implies T" means that we need to make (some, no) further assumption when deducing T from S. (Which)?

---

no

5.   "Besides the relations between S and T, Logic is not concerned

with their actual truth. "   True/False?

True.

6. (Read carefully)
It is sometimes said that L o g i c is concerned with the <u>form</u> of
statements rather than with their <u>meaning</u>.
Thus when we say that
                    "Jones is an unmarried male"
            implies "Jones is unmarried",
what we say does not depend on the meanings of the words "Jones",
"unmarried" and "male" but only on the fact that they are arranged
in a certain pattern.
We might just as well have said that
                            "X is AB"
                implies "X is A".
Or we could have used nonsense-words, as in saying that
            "Robinson is a frumptious greeble"
        implies "Robinson is frumptious".
If we were to say that
            "Mrs. Smith is a happy housewife"
        implies "Mrs. Smith is happy,
would what we say be of the same <u>form</u> as the earlier examples, or
not?

Yes, it would.

7.   Does "All mimmeltoes are elatical" imply "All fannish mimmeltoes are elatical?" and is this the same as saying that "All policemen are happy" implies "All married policemen are happy"?

Yes (<u>both questions</u>).

8. We shall use the letters "S", "T", "U", "V" to stand for
<u>statements</u> and the letters "A", "B", "C" for terms which occur
within statements. In its logical sense, "implies" is used to indicate

18

a relation between two (statements, terms). (Which?)

---

statements.

9. When S implies T or when T implies S we say that there is a relation of <u>implication</u> between S and T.
Is there a relation of implication between "Smith is male" and "Smith is a father"?

Yes.

10. "Jones is a bachelor" implies "Jones is male" but does "Jones is male" imply "Jones is a bachelor"?

No.

11. Is it possible for S to imply T but T not imply S?

Yes.

12. We shall use the symbol "$\rightarrow$" to mean "implies"
"S $\rightarrow$ T" means "S implies T".
does "S $\rightarrow$ T" mean the same as "T $\rightarrow$ S"?

No.

13. Consider the following statements:

S: "Smith is male and has at least one son or daughter"
T: "Smith is a father"
Which of the following are true: S $\rightarrow$ T? T $\rightarrow$ S? Both?

Both.

14. Is the following statement true: "If S implies T, T may imply S, but need not"?

Yes.

15. Is the following statement also true: "If S does not imply T, T may imply S, but need not"?

Yes.

16. A relation is called <u>symmetrical</u> if, whenever one thing has it to another, the second also has it to the first. The relation "cousin of" is . . . .

---

symmetrical.

17. The relation "father of" is not symmetrical. The relation of implication (is, is not) symmetrical.

---

is not

18. Does "S ⟶ T" imply "T ⟶ S"?

No.

19. Is it possible for "S ⟶ T" and "T ⟶ S" both to be true?

Yes.

20. Consider the four cases:

   (1) S ⟶ T
   (2) T ⟶ S
   (3) Both S ⟶ T and T ⟶ S
   (4) Neither S ⟶ T nor T ⟶ S.

20

Write the number or numbers (1), (2), (3) or (4) of the cases in which we would say there is a relation of implication between S and T.

---

(1), (2), (3)

21.   Consider the statements

S: "No grampangs are windiddlies"
T: "There is nothing that is both a windiddly and a grampang"

S → T?   T → S?   Both?   Neither?

Both.

22.   Clearly it is not always enough to know just that the relation between two statements is one of implication. We need, that is, to know which statement implies which, and whether they both imply one another. Let us deal with this last possibility first: If there is a relation of implication both ways between S and T, we shall say that S and T are equivalent. Consider the four cases

(1)   S → T
(2)   T → S
(3)   Both S → T and T → S
(4)   Neither S → T nor T → S.

Write the number or numbers of the cases in which we would say that S and T are equivalent.

---

(3)

23.   When two statements are equivalent we shall also say there is a relation of equivalence. Is the relation of equivalence symmetrical?

Yes.

24.   "The relation of equivalence is a special case of the relation

21

of implication." True/False?

True.

25. If S is equivalent to T then "S $\rightarrow$ T" is (true, false).

---

true.

26. If S does not imply T and T does not imply S can S and T be equivalent?

No.

27. We shall sometimes use the sign "$\leftrightarrow$" to mean "is equivalent to".

Does "S $\leftrightarrow$ T" mean the same as "T $\leftrightarrow$ S"?

Yes.

28. (Read carefully)
If S implies T but T <u>does not imply</u> S we shall say that the <u>relation of S to T is superimplication</u>, or that <u>S has the relation of super-implication to T</u>.

It should be noticed that in the case of the relation of super-implication it is important to specify in which <u>order</u> S and T are taken. (In the other order, the relation is called <u>subimplication</u>.)
Is the relation of superimplication symmetrical?

No.

29. The relation of
         "John is a bachelor"
        to "John is male"
        is . . . .

---

superimplication.

22

30. The relation of

"No doctors are dentists"
to "No dentists are doctors"
is . . . .

---

equivalence.

31. The relation of

"All wogglies are gombular"
to "All shushful wogglies are gombular"
is. . . . .

---

superimplication.

32. Is it true that it is impossible for two statements to have the relation of superimplication and the relation of equivalence at the same time?

Yes.

33. The relation of

"All wogglies are gombular"
to "No woggly is non-gombular"
is . . . .

---

equivalence.

34. As we have said, subimplication is the relation that S has to T when S does not imply T but T does imply S.

When the relation of S to T is subimplication what is the relation of T to S?

Superimplication.

35. Let us use " $\nrightarrow$ " to mean "does not imply".

In which of the following cases, (1) or (2), does S have the relation of subimplication to T?

   (1) S $\longrightarrow$ T; T $\nrightarrow$ S?
   (2) S $\nrightarrow$ T; T $\longrightarrow$ S?

(Write the number)

---

(2)

36. The relation of
        "Mrs. Smith is a housewife"
        to "Mrs. Smith is a happy housewife"
        is . . . .

---

subimplication.

37. "There are just three kinds of implication: superimplication, subimplication and equivalence."
Right/Wrong?

Right.

38. If S has the relation of subimplication to T, can T have the relation of subimplication to S?

No.

39. The relation of "Tom is taller than Harold" to "Tom is taller than Harold and John" is. . . . .

---

subimplication.

40. The relation of "Some bears are marsupials" to "Some marsupials are bears" is . . . .

---

equivalence.

41.   The relation of "To get to the other side of the Bay it is necessary to drive round" to "It is not possible to get to the other side of the Bay without driving round" is ∴..........

---

equivalence.

42.   The relation of "All transparent plastics are good insulators" to "Everything transparent is a good insulator" is ....

---

subimplication.

43.   The relation of "Platinum has approximately the same coefficient of expansion as crown glass" to "Crown glass has approximately the same coefficient of expansion as platinum" is ....

---

equivalence.

END OF CHAPTER 2

Chapter 3: Contradiction and Contrariety

In this chapter the concept of the <u>negation</u> of a statement is introduced, and a distinction is drawn between the true negation or <u>contradictory</u> of a statement and <u>contraries</u> of the statement.

1. Logical relations, in the sense in which we use the word, hold not between <u>terms</u> but between . . . .

---

statements.

2. When a statement S implies another statement T but T does not imply S, the relation of S to T is . . . .
and the relation of T to S is . . . .

---

superimplication
subimplication (<u>in that order</u>)

3. What is the relation of
            "Jones has a brother who has children"
        to "Jones is someone's uncle"?

Superimplication.

4. We do not normally bother to ask what logical relation a statement has to <u>itself</u>; but, if we did, what would the answer have to be?

Equivalence.

26

5. If S does not imply T, does it follow that T does not imply S?

___

No.

6. Is the relation "does not imply" symmetrical?

___

No.

7. Consider the four cases:
(1) $S \rightarrow T$, $T \rightarrow S$
(2) $S \rightarrow T$, $T \nrightarrow S$
(3) $S \nrightarrow T$, $T \rightarrow S$
(4) $S \nrightarrow T$, $T \nrightarrow S$

With which case or cases have we not yet associated the name of a logical relation?
(Write the number or numbers, or "None")

___

(4)

8. (Read carefully)
In case (4) of the last example there is no implication relation between S and T. However, there may still be a relation of some other kind. Consider the statements:
S: "There is cheese in the fridge", and
T: "There is no cheese in the fridge".
Here we would say that T contradicts S (or, T is the contradictory of S; or, S and T are contradictories).
"If S is the contradictory of T, T is the contradictory of S."
True/False?

___

True.

9. Can two contradictory statements ever both be true?

___

No.

10. If S and T are contradictories, is it possible that there should be an implication relation between them?

No.

11. The contradictory of a statement is also sometimes called its negation. This is because to transform a statement into its contradictory it is generally sufficient to insert the word "not" (or the words "does not", etc.) next to the main verb; or, if these words are already there, to remove them.
The negation of "The South Pacific Ocean circulates counter-clockwise" is
"The South Pacific Ocean .... counter-clockwise".

---

does not circulate

12. (Read carefully)
Sometimes, however, the negation (or contradictory) of a statement is formed by changing "Some" to "No", or vice versa; or by changing "Sometimes" to "Never", or vice versa.
The negation of "I have nothing in my pocket" could be expressed "I do not have nothing in my pocket", but it would be more natural to express it "I have .... in my pocket".

---

something

13. In symbols we write the negation (or contradictory) of S in the form "-S".
If T is the negation of S, T is equivalent to ....

-S.

14. If S begins with the word "All" we generally form -S by changing this to "Not all". A form such as "All As are not Bs" should be avoided, since it is ambiguous and can mean either
　　(1) "Not all As are Bs", or
　　(2) "All As are non-Bs".

28

Which of these is the correct negation of "All As are Bs"?
(Write the number)

---

(1)

15. When in doubt, a good general method of negating a statement
is to prefix it with the phrase "It is not the case that".
The reason this is a good method is that it usually gives quite clearly
a statement which is .... when the original one is ...., and vice
versa.

---

false .... true
(in either order)

16. Is the relation of "All radios use crystal diodes" to "Not all
radios use crystal diodes" one of superimplication, subimplication,
equivalence, or none of these?

None of these.

17. When two statements are contradictories the logical relation
between them is called contradiction.
When the relation between S and T is contradiction and S is true, T
must be .....

---

false.

18. The relation of S to -S is ....

---

contradiction.

19. What is the relation of "Tai always eats with chopsticks" to
"Tai does not always eat with chopsticks"?

Contradiction.

29

20.   What is the relation of
              "Not all adults are voters"
         to "It is not the case that all adults are voters"?

(Superimplication/Subimplication/Equivalence/Contradiction/None
of these)

Equivalence.

21.   The statement that has the relation of contradiction to "Marine
oil-drilling is not always hazardous" is "Marine oil-drilling is . . . . . .
hazardous".

---

always

22.   If two statements do not stand in an implication relation, do
they have to stand in a relation of contradiction?

No.

23.   What is the relation of
              "Not all Indo- European languages are inflected"
         to "Not all inflected languages are Indo-European"?

(Superimplication/Subimplication/ Equivalence/Contradiction/ None
of these)

None of these.

24.   "If S and T are contradictories they cannot both be true and
they cannot both be false." True/False?

True.

25.   Could the statements "All bulldogs are vicious" and "No bulldogs
are vicious" both be false?

Yes.

26. (Read carefully)
We have seen that the negation of "All As are Bs" is "Not all As are Bs". But the latter statement is different from "No As are Bs"; and it follows that "All As are Bs" and "No As are Bs" do not stand in a relation of true contradiction.

"All As are Bs" and "No As are Bs" can both be false, namely if some As are Bs and others not.

When two statements cannot both be true but can both be false, they are called contraries.

The statements "Joan is tall and fair" and "Joan is tall and dark" are . . . .

---

contraries.

27. Contraries can both be . . . . . but . . . . . . both be . . . .

---

false . . . cannot . . true.

28. Two statements in the relation of contradiction (that is, which are contradictories) cannot both be . . . . and . . . . . . both be false.

---

true . . . cannot

29. Jones must be either present or absent. The statements "Jones is present" and "Jones is absent" are (contradictories, contraries).

---

contradictories.

30. Smith could be an undergraduate student or he could be a graduate student or he could be neither. The statements "Smith is a graduate student" and "Smith is an undergraduate student" are (contradictories, contraries).

---

contraries.

31. Contraries have to one another the relation of <u>contrariety</u>. (Say: contra-RIety).

The relation of "There is a large piece of cheese in the fridge" to "There is no cheese in the fridge" is ....

---

contrariety.

32. The population of New Zealand could be more than three million, could be less than three million, and could conceivably be exactly three million.
The relation of
      "The population of N.Z. is over 3m."
      to "The population of N.Z. is under 3m."
      is .:..........

---

contrariety.

33. When S and T are contraries, they can both be false and hence some third statement U, contrary to both of them, may be true.
A statement contrary to
      "John can run faster than Mary"
and also to "John and Mary can run each as fast as the other"
is "Mary .... John".

---

can run faster than

34. A statement contrary to both "No As are Bs" and "At least one A is a B but not all are" is "... As are Bs".

All

35. What is the relation of
      "No reptiles are rodents"
      to "No rodents are reptiles"?

Equivalence.

36.   If S and T stand in the relation of equivalence, S and -T . . . . . .
both be true and . . . . . . both be false.

---

cannot . . . cannot

37.   What is the relation of "It is certain that every event has a
cause" to "It is possible that there is or was or will be at least one
uncaused event"?
(Superimplication/ Subimplication/ Equivalence/ Contradiction/ Con -
trariety/ None of these)

Contradiction.

38.   What is the relation of
        "All metals denser than lead are radioactive"
     to "No metals denser than lead are radioactive"?

Contrariety.

39.   What is the relation of
        "There are just twenty countries in Europe"
     to "There are more than twenty countries in Europe"?

Contrariety.

40.   Contradictories can't both be true and . . . . both be false.

---

can't

END OF CHAPTER 3

Chapter 4: Subcontrariety and Indifference

In this chapter the remaining two of the seven logical relations are introduced, and a systematic classification of them is made.

1.   The negation of a statement S is true when S is ..... and ..... when S is ....

---

false ... false .. true
(in that order)

2.   The negation of a statement containing the word "somewhere" can usually be formed by changing this word to "....... ".

"nowhere".

3.   The relation of
"All mimmical wigglies are bilbulous" to
"Not all mimmical wigglies are bilbulous" is ....

---

contradiction.

4.   When two statements can't both be true the relation between them is either .... or ....

---

contradiction .. contrariety.

5.   The distinction between contradictories and contraries is that whereas contradictories ..... both be false, contraries ... both be false.

---

can't .... can
(in that order)

6.   The relation of
"All collicles are orlacious" to
"There are no orlacious collicles" is ....

---

contrariety.

7.   When S and T are contradictories and S is false, T must be (true, false). (Which?)

---

true.

8.   If S and T can't both be true but can both be false the relation between them is ....

---

contrariety.

9.   (Read carefully)
When two statements can both be true they are neither contradictories nor contraries. If, however, they cannot both be false they are called subcontraries.

Contraries   : can't both be true
                  can both be false

Contradictories: can't both be true
                  can't both be false

Subcontraries : can both be true
                  can't both be false.

The statements "At least one spiral nebula is receding" and "At least one spiral nebula is not receding" are . . . .

---

subcontraries.

    10.   If two statements can't both be true their negations can't both be false. If S and T are contraries, -S and -T are . . . .

---

subcontraries.

    11.   Subcontraries stand in the relation of <u>subcontrariety</u>. (Say: sub-contra-RIety).
The relation of
            "John is not taller than Bill" to
            "Bill is not taller than John" is. . . . .

---

subcontrariety.

    12.   The relation of
            "Offshore oil is being worked near Sydney" to
            "There is no offshore oil near Sydney" is . . . .

---

contrariety.

    13.   The relation of "It is not the case that experiments have indicated that cancer is due to a virus" to "There have been experiments on the cause of cancer" is . . . .

---

subcontrariety.

    14.   What is the relation of
        "We know that there is life on Venus"
      to "We know that there is no life on Venus"?
(Superimplication/Subimplication/Equivalence/Contradiction/Contrariety/Subcontrariety/None of these)

Contrariety.

15. What is the relation of
     "Reading the works of Winston Churchill is not forbidden" to
     "Reading the works of Winston Churchill is not compulsory"?

Subcontrariety.

16. We have now introduced <u>six</u> different logical relations, in two
groups of three. The group "contradiction - contrariety - subcontrariety" in some way matches the earlier group "equivalence -
superimplication - subimplication". What is the relation of
     "Logic is at least a little easier than Mathematics"
  to "Logic is much easier than Mathematics"?

Subimplication.

17. Consider the four following statements:
         S: "All spiral nebulae are receding"
         T: "No spiral nebulae are receding"
         U: "At least one spiral nebula is receding"
         V: "At least one spiral nebula is not receding".

What are the relations

         (a) of S to T?
         (b) of S to U?
         (c) of S to V?
         (d) of T to U?
         (e) of T to V?
         (f) of U to V?

(a) contrariety   (d) contradiction
(b) superimplication   (e) superimplication
(c) contradiction   (f) subcontrariety.

18. In the previous example, granted that the relation of S to U is
superimplication, what is the relation of U to S?

Subimplication.

19. (Read carefully)

When two statements S and T have none of the six relations already introduced, we shall say that they are <u>indifferent</u>, or that the logical relation between them is <u>indifference.</u>

In all cases of implication relations, the <u>truth</u> of one statement implies the <u>truth</u> of the other.

In all cases of contradiction, contrariety or subcontrariety, there is a restriction on whether the statements can be <u>true together</u>, or <u>false together</u>.

In the case of indifference, the <u>truth</u> or <u>falsity</u> of one statement does not tell us anything at all about the <u>truth</u> or <u>falsity</u> of the other.

When S and T are indifferent, what is the relation:

     (a) of T to S?
     (b) of -S to -T?
     (c) of S to -T?

(a) indifference (b) indifference (c) indifference.

20. All bachelors are males. Are all males bachelors?

No.

21. Does "All kangaroos are marsupials"
imply "All marsupials are kangaroos"?

No.

22. (Read carefully)

Together with superimplication, subimplication, equivalence, contradiction, contrariety and subcontrariety, indifference makes up the list of seven traditionally recognised logical relations.

In the vast majority of cases, two statements chosen at random will, of course, be indifferent. In particular, statements on different subject-matter -- such as "All bachelors are happy" and "There is a spider on the wall" -- are bound to be indifferent. But we have also seen that apparently closely related statements can be indifferent too. What is the relation of

38

"All snakes are egglayers"
to "All egglayers are snakes "?

Indifference.

23. (Read carefully)
By a "logical relation" we mean -- at least so far as this course is concerned -- a relation between two statements that is definable solely in terms of the possibilities of truth and falsity of these statements in combination. It would, of course, be possible to use the words "logical relation" more broadly. For example, "All Bs are As" is sometimes called the converse of "All As are Bs", simply because it arises from the interchange of the two terms. But we shall not be concerned with the "converse" relation as such in this course.
What is the logical relation, in the sense in which we use the word in this course, between "All As are Bs" and "All Bs are As"?

Indifference.

24. What is the relation of
"At least one A is not a B"
to "At least one B is not an A"?

Indifference.

25. Indifference is sometimes a little difficult to tell from subcontrariety. The test is, however, whether the two statements can both be false. If they cannot, the relation (apart from other possibilities) must be ....

---

subcontrariety.

26. In cases of difficulty we can determine the logical relation between a pair of statements S and T by systematically asking ourselves a sequence of "yes-no" questions about them.
Consider, for example, the question "Can S and T both be true?" If the answer to this question is "No", which relations are singled

out as the possible ones?

Contradiction, contrariety
(in either order)

27.   If the question asked were "Can they both be false?", and the answer were "No", what would be the possible relations?

Contradiction, subcontrariety
(in either order)

28.   If the question asked were "Does either imply the other?", and the answer were "No", what would be the possible relations?

Contradiction, contrariety, subcontrariety, indifference
(in any order)

29.   In the case of the following "question-tree", what is the relation corresponding with the end of each branch?

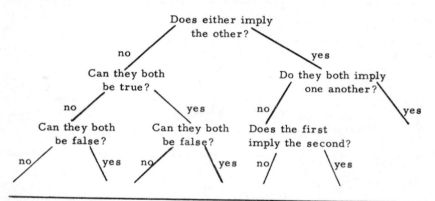

Contradiction,   contrariety,   subcontrariety,   indifference,
subimplication,   superimplication,   equivalence
(in that order)

40

30.   If S has the relation of contrariety to T, which of the following possibilities is or are definitely excluded?

  (1) S and T both true?
  (2) S true and T false?
  (3) S false and T true?
  (4) S and T both false?

(Write the number or numbers, or "None")

---

(1)

31.   If S has the relation of superimplication to T, which of the above possibilities (1) - (4) is definitely excluded?
(Write the number or numbers, or "None")

---

(2)

32.   If S and T are in the relation of e q u i v a l e n c e which of the possibilities (1) - (4) are definitely excluded?
(Write the number or numbers, or "None")

---

(2), (3)

33.   What is the relation of
        "Text books are rarely, if ever, good literature"
      to "Text books are never good literature"?

Subimplication.

34.   What is the relation of
            "Most logicians are pedants (and perhaps all are)"
        to "Some logicians are pedants and some are not"?

Indifference.

35.   What is the relation of
                     "S and T are contraries"
             to S itself?

Indifference.

   36.   In general, what is the relation of
                  "The logical relation of S to T is X"
             to S itself?

Indifference.

   37.   Does knowledge of logical relations ever by itself give us any
   knowledge of the truth or falsity of the individual statements
   concerned?

No.

END OF CHAPTER 4

Chapter 5: Ambiguity and Empty Terms

This chapter deals with some special kinds of ambiguity which affect the logical relations that statements may have. The student may omit this chapter in order to proceed to Part II if he wishes, but should work through this chapter before proceeding to Part III.

1. Two statements are contraries if they .... both be true but .... both be false.

---

can't .... can
(in that order)

2. The relations of contrariety and contradiction (between two statements) are both such that if one statement is .... the other is .....

---

true .... false
(in that order)

3. What is the relation of "All variegated azaleas bloom in winter" to "Not all variegated azaleas bloom in winter"?

Contradiction.

4. (Read carefully)
The case of "All As are Bs" and "No As are Bs" is complicated by the fact that we must allow for the possibility that there do not exist

43

any As at all. We would normally ignore this possibility and, if we do, the statements are contraries. But it is not clear what we should say about examples such as "All unicorns are four-legged" and "No unicorns are four-legged", for perhaps, if there are no unicorns, these should both be regarded as true. If they <u>can</u> both be true, they are not contraries.

Let us suppose that it is certain there are no unicorns. In this case, "No unicorns are four-legged" is presumably <u>true</u> -- we shall say it is "vacuously true", and that the term "unicorn" is <u>empty</u> or <u>vacuous</u>.

Which of the following simple or complex terms are, in common knowledge or belief, empty?

(1) five-sided square?
(2) centaur?
(3) rhinoceros?
(4) non-conducting metal?

(Write the number or numbers, or "None")

---

(1), (2), (4)

5. In traditional logic it was usually assumed without question that any term used could be taken as <u>non-empty</u> and that the relation of, say, "All As are Bs" to other statements could be worked out without allowing for the fact that there may be no As.

In traditional logic, would "All As are Bs" have been taken to imply "There is at least one A that is a B"?

Yes.

6. Alternatively, however, we may take into account the possibility that A <u>may</u> be empty. Under these circumstances we regard "All As are Bs" as really meaning "There are <u>no</u> As that are <u>not</u> Bs", and hence as being automatically true if there are no As. Similarly we regard "No As are Bs" as meaning "There is nothing which is both an A and a B", and hence as also being automatically true if there are no As.

If we assume that the terms used are <u>non</u>-empty, can "All unicorns are four-legged" and "No unicorns are four-legged" both

44

be true?

No.

    7.   What if we permit the terms to be empty?

Yes.

    8.   If we assume that there are As, "All As are Bs" will _imply_ "At least one A is a B"; but if there may be no As, the first may be true and the second false.

What, if empty terms are _not_ permitted, is the relation of "All unicorns are friendly" to "There is at least one friendly unicorn"? And what if empty terms _are_ permitted?

Superimplication, indifference
(in that order)

    9.   When we compare "All As are Bs with, say, "No As are Bs" we do not need to know whether the term A is _actually_ empty: this is, in any case, not usually a matter of Logic.   But if the term A may be empty, we shall have to allow that the two statements _may_ possibly both be true.

What, if empty terms are not permitted, is the relation of
        "All metals denser than lead are radioactive"
    to "No metals denser than lead are radioactive"?

Contrariety.

    10.   If empty terms are permitted and if "All As are Bs" and "No As are Bs" are taken as automatically _true_ if there are no As (that is, as "vacuously true"), the statements can both be true and can both be false and are . . . .

indifferent.

11.   What, if empty terms are permitted, is the relation of "All Martians have X-ray vision" to (a) "No Martians have X-ray vision" and to (b) "At least one Martian has X-ray vision"?

(a) Indifference, (b) Indifference.

12.   If empty terms are not permitted, the relation of
"No gonchbills have long tweedles"
to "Not all gonchbills have long tweedles"
is . . . .

---

superimplication.

13.   And what if empty terms are permitted?

Indifference.

14.   Consider the following diagram, known as a "square of opposition":

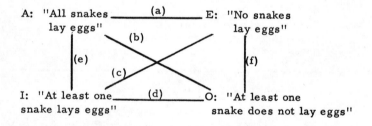

The letters A, E, I and O traditionally represent the <u>forms</u> of statements: A is <u>universal affirmative</u>, E is <u>universal negative</u>, I is <u>particular affirmative</u>, O is <u>particular negative</u>. The affirmative ones are given by the first two vowels in the Latin word "AffIrmo" and the negative ones by the vowels in "nEgO".

46

Assuming no empty terms, what are the relations corresponding with the lines (a), (b), (c), (d), (e), (f)?
(In the case of Implication say which implies which.)

(a) contrariety   (d) subcontrariety
(b) contradiction   (e) implication, A ⟶ I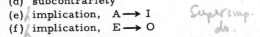
(c) contradiction   (f) implication, E ⟶ O

15. Now suppose empty terms may occur. If "A" is empty "All As are Bs" is interpreted as "There are no As that are not Bs" and hence as being automatically . . . .

---

true.

16. If empty terms may occur, "All As are Bs" and "No As are Bs" may both be (vacuously) true. Hence, what is the relation of "All enfranchised peers vote Conservative" to "No enfranchised peers vote Conservative"?

Indifference.

17. What are the possible alternative relations of "All present day Sydney trams are steam-driven" to "At least one present-day Sydney tram is steam-driven",
            (a) without allowing for emptiness of terms
            (b) allowing for such emptiness?

(a) Superimplication, (b) Indifference.

18. Consider the four following statements:
        S: All moas fly
        T: No moas fly
        U: At least one moa flies
        V: At least one moa does not fly.

Allowing that there may be no moas, between which pairs of state - ments is there a relation other than indifference, and what is it?

S and V, contradiction
T and U, contradiction
(pairs in either order, letters within pairs in either order)

19. Consider the four statements from the previous example arranged in a "square of opposition" as follows:

What relation is appropriate to the sides of the square? And what relation is appropriate to the diagonals?

Indifference, contradiction
(in that order)

20. What is the relation of
"It is possible that Alexander the Great did not penetrate
to the Ganges"
to "It is not possible that Alexander the Great penetrated to
the Ganges"?

Subimplication.

21. If empty terms are permitted, what is the relation of "All true democracies are efficient" to "There is no true democracy"?

Subimplication.

22.   "All and only metals are conductors" means the same as "All metals are conductors and all conductors are metals". True/False?

True.

23.   (Read carefully)
When we say "Only As are Bs" we <u>may</u>, or we <u>may not</u>, imply that every A is a B. For example, "Only ocean-going vessels carry lifeboats" seems to imply that <u>all</u> ocean-going vessels carry lifeboats; though a little reflection might make us doubt this.

In other cases it is clear that there is no such implication: "Only adults are voters" is true, but does not imply "All adults are voters", which is false since such people as convicted criminals are denied the vote.

What are the two possibilities regarding the relation of "Only As are Bs" to "All As are Bs"?

Indifference, superimplication
(<u>in either order</u>)

24.   (Read carefully)
What "Only As are Bs" <u>does</u> imply is "All Bs are As". For example, "Only adults are voters" implies "All voters are adults".

The statement "Only ocean-going vessels carry lifeboats" (implies, does not imply) "All vessels that carry lifeboats are ocean-going". (Which?)

---

implies

25.   "Only adults are voters" does not imply "All adults are voters". What, then, is the relation of "Only adults are voters" to "All voters are adults"?

(Superimplication/Subimplication/Equivalence/None of these)

Equivalence.

49

26. "If 'Only As are Bs' is understood in the sense in which it implies that all As are Bs, it is equivalent to 'All and only As are Bs'." True/False?

True.

27. Compare the phrase "All and only" with the phrase "if and only if". Does "A bear is marsupial if and only if it is Australian" mean the same as "All and only Australian bears are marsupial bears"?

Yes.

28. When a statement is clearly ambiguous we should, if necessary, allow that there may be <u>two or more possible</u> logical relations that it may have to some other statement. In such a case we should give all possible alternatives.

The word "student" may or may not include schoolchildren. What are the possible relations of

"All students have heard of Archimedes"
to "All schoolchildren have heard of Archimedes"?

Superimplication, indifference
(<u>in either order</u>)

29. A statement of the form "All As are Bs", as used in Logic, is usually intended to refer to past and future As as well as present: that is, it means "All As, past, present and future, were, are and will be Bs". Sometimes, however, statements of the form "All As are Bs" simply mean "All As are Bs at the present time".

What are the possible relations of "All swans are white or black" to "No one will ever breed a brindle swan"?

Superimplication, indifference
(<u>in either order</u>)

30. The word "Some" is usually used by logicians in the sense of "At least some, and possibly all"; but sometimes, especially when

emphasised, can mean "Some but not all", that is, "Some and only some". What are the possible relations of "Not all peerages are hereditary" to "Some peerages are hereditary"?

Subimplication, indifference
(in either order)

31. Consider the two statements
$$S: \text{ "All As are Bs"}$$
$$T: \text{ "All Bs are As".}$$
The statement "Only As are Bs" definitely implies one of the two, and only possibly implies the other. Which is the one it definitely implies?

"All Bs are As"

32. What are the possible relations of
"Not all students have heard of Archimedes"
to "Not all schoolboys have heard of Archimedes"?

Subimplication, indifference.

33. What is the relation of
"Reptiles cannot fly"
to "In prehistoric times there were flying reptiles"?

(Give alternatives, depending as the first statement does, or does not, include prehistoric times.)

Contrariety, indifference.

34. What is the relation of
"I always like going to the theatre"
to "Everybody always likes going to live theatre"?

(Give alternatives, depending as the word "theatre", does or does not include cinemas.)

Indifference, subimplication.

35. What is the relation of

"Some of the distinction made by logicians are of no consequence"
to "Some of the distinctions made by logicians are of the highest
consequence"

if "some" is interpreted as not excluding "all"? What would it be if
"some" were interpreted as "some and only some"?

Indifference
(both cases)

END OF CHAPTER 5

END OF PART 1

Part 2
The Logic of Unanalysed Statements

This part deals with the so-called "propositional calculus", in which statements are represented by letters (such as "S", "T", ..) and we explore the way in which compound statements can be made up using "and", "or" and "not", and the logical properties of such compounds.

It is assumed that the reader has a grasp of the material in chapters 1-4 of Part 1.

Chapter 6: Negation and Conjunction

Negation was introduced in chapter 3; conjunction is introduced in this chapter, and a start is made on exploring the logical relations between compound statements.

1.   Let us start by revising what we said earlier about negation. The negation of a statement S is written "-S" (pronounced "not S") and it is the statement which is true when S is false, and false when S is true.
    In the simplest case the negation of a statement is formed by inserting the word "not" (or the words "does not", etc.).
    The negation of "Cairo is in Egypt" is "Cairo ...."

---

is not in Egypt

2.   "If S is the negation of T, T is the negation of S." True/False?

True.

3. The negation of
              "John does not like ballet"
              is "John . . . ."

". . . . likes ballet", <u>or</u> ". . . .does like ballet"

4. Sometimes, however, the negation of a statement is formed by changing "Some" to "No" or <u>vice versa</u>, or in some other way like this.
Which of the following is the negation of "Mathematicians sometimes make mistakes"?

     (1) "Mathematicians do not always make mistakes"?
     (2) "Mathematicians sometimes make no mistakes"?
     (3) "Mathematicians never make mistakes"?
(Write the number)

---

(3)

5. The negation is false when the original statement is true, and true when the original statement is false. Which of the following is the negation of "There is always someone about the University"?

     (1) "There is sometimes no one about at the University"?
     (2) "There is never no one about at the University"?
     (3) "There is never anyone about at the University"?
     (Write the number)

---

(1)

6. There may, of course, be different formulations of the negation of a statement. Which of the following are negations of "All Frenchmen are talkative"?

     (1) "Some Frenchmen are talkative"?
     (2) "Some Frenchman, at least, is not talkative"?
     (3) "Frenchmen are not all talkative"?
     (4) "There exist quite a few non-talkative Frenchmen"?
     (5) "It is not the case that all Frenchmen are talkative"?

---

(2), (3), (5)

    7.   The logical relation of S to -S is . . . .

---

contradiction.

    8.   --S is the negation of -S.
What is the relation of --S to S?

Equivalence.

    9.   If S is equivalent to -T what is the relation of -S to T?

Equivalence.

    10.   We are now in a position to introduce some other concepts to go with negation.

    In the statement "There is a chair and a table in my room" there are two component statements, namely the statements "There is a chair in my room" and "There is a table in my room". The statement as a whole is called the <u>conjunction</u> of the two component statements. The conjunction "S and T" of S and T is true if and only if S and T are both true.

    The conjunction of two statements (implies, is implied by) either separately. (Which?)

---

implies

    11.   We shall write the conjunction "S and T" in the form "S.T" (or sometimes just "ST"). What is the relation of S.T to T.S?

Equivalence.

55

12.   The word "and" usually, but not always, indicates a conjunction.   In which of the following cases is there a conjunction of two statements?

    (1) Tom and Mary have red hair.
    (2) Tom and Mary are together.
    (3) There are 27 men and women in the room.
    (4) There are 14 men and 13 women in the room.
    (5) Smith and Jones are 6'2" and 5'9" respectively.

(Write the number or numbers)

---

(1),   (4),   (5)

13.   We can form the conjunction of three or more statements in the form "S.T.U", "S.T.U.V" and so on.   The triple conjunction can be considered as the conjunction of S.T with U, that is, as
$$(S.T).U$$
or alternatively as the conjunction of S with T.U; that is, as
$$S.(T.U)$$
but these two forms are equivalent and so we do not need the brackets. How many component statements are there in the statement "Smith and Jones are happy and successful"?

Four.

14.   The conjunction S.T can be defined as that statement which is <u>true</u> when S and T are <u>both true</u>, but <u>false</u> if either one of them is <u>false</u>.   It follows that the conjunction S.T.U is <u>true</u> when S, T and U are <u>all true</u>, but <u>false</u> if any one (or more) of them is <u>false</u>.
If S is true, does it follow that S.T is true?
If S.T is true, does it follow that S is true?

No
Yes
(<u>in that order</u>)

15.   Sometimes we use the word "but" instead of the word "and", to indicate opposition of some kind between the component statements;

56

for example, in "Warships are grey but liners are usually white".
However, there is no <u>logical opposition</u> between "Warships are grey"
and "Liners are usually white" -- they are not contradictories or
contraries -- and so, for most purposes, we can treat the compound
statement simply as a conjunction.

What is the logical relation of "Speech is silver but silence is golden"
(a) to "Speech is silver"?   (b) to "Silence is golden"?

Superimplication
(<u>in both cases</u>)

16.   If S and T are true and U is false, which of the following are
true?

$$(1) \quad -S.T \ ?$$
$$(2) \quad S.-U \ ?$$
$$(3) \quad -U.S.-T \ ?$$
$$(4) \quad T.S \ ?$$

(Write the number or numbers, or "None")

---

(2), (4)

17.   We can also negate a conjunction. Thus "$-(S.T)$" means "Not
both S and T", that is "It is not the case that S and T are both true".
The brackets are necessary to distinguish it from "$-S.T$", which
means "S is false and T is true".

If S means "There is butter in the fridge" and T means "There
is cheese in the fridge", which of the following represents "$-(S.T)$"?

(1) "There is no butter or cheese in the fridge"?
(2) "There is no butter and no cheese in the fridge"?
(3) "There is not both butter and cheese in the fridge"?

(Write the number)

---

(3)

18.   Does $-(S.T)$ mean the same as $-S.-T$?

No.

19.   If S means "It will rain" and T means "We shall go to the beach",
write a formula representing "It will rain and we shall not go to the
beach".

S. -T

20.   With the same meanings for S and T, write a formula representing "It is not the case both that it will rain and that we shall go to
the beach".

-(S. T)

21.   If S means "Smith is present" and T means "Jones is happy",
the formula -(S. -T) means "It is not the case both that . . . .
and that . . . ."

Smith is present . . . . Jones is not happy

22.   We noted that the conjunction of two statements implies each
of them separately.   That is, S. T implies S, and similarly S. T
implies T.
Using the arrow-symbol " ⟶ " we can write these implications
$$S. T \longrightarrow S$$
$$S. T \longrightarrow T$$
An implication can be <u>valid</u> or <u>invalid</u>.   Context 2.13 , 8.1
Is the implication S. -T ⟶ -T valid?

Yes.

23.   If S is true and T false, -(S. T) is . . . .

---

true.

24.   Say which of the following implications are valid:

58

(1) S. -T $\longrightarrow$ -(S. T)?
(2) -S. -T $\longrightarrow$ -(S. T)?
(3) -S. T $\longrightarrow$ -(S. T)?

(Write the number or numbers, or "None")

---

(1), (2), (3)

25. In which of the following cases is -(S. T) true?

(1) When S and T are both true?
(2) When S is true and T false?
(3) When S is false and T true?
(4) When S and T are both false?

(Write the number or numbers)

---

(2), (3), (4)

26. In which of the same four cases are S and -(S. T) both true?
(Write the number or numbers, or "None")

---

(2)

27. We shall generally assume, when we use letters "S", "T",
"U", ... to represent unspecified statements, that the relation
between any two such statements is indifference.
However, relations between c o m p o u n d statements are often not
indifference.
The relation of S. T to S is ....

---

superimplication.

28. The relation of S. T to T. S is ....

---

equivalence.

29.   The relation of S to -S is ....

---

contradiction.

   30.   Now let us construct examples of the other logical relations.
Two statements are <u>contraries</u> when they can't both be true but can
both be false.
Two statements are <u>subcontraries</u> when they can't both be false but
can both be true.
The relation of S. T to S. -T is ....

---

contrariety.

   31.   The relation of S to -(S. T) is ....

---

subcontrariety.

   32.   The relation of -S to S. -T is ....

---

contrariety.

END OF CHAPTER 6

Chapter 7: Disjunction

In this chapter we introduce a symbol for "or", and relate it to conjunction and negation.

1. The negation -S of a statement S is defined as a statement which is true when S is ....., and ....

---

false .... false when S is true.

2. The conjunction S.T of two statements S and T is defined as a statement which is true when S and T ...., but false otherwise.

---

are true, or are both true

3. Negation and conjunction are called truth-functions, because they are defined simply in terms of truth and falsehood, relatively to the truth and falsehood of the component statements.
Other compounds using negation and conjunction may also be described as truth-functions. Thus, S.-T is a truth-function of S and T because it is a statement which is true when S is .... and T is ....., but false otherwise.

---

true ... false
(in that order)

4. Write a specification, in truth-functional terms, of the compound

61

statement S.T.U:
It is true when ....
and false when ....

(In suitable words:)
....S, T and U are all true, ..any one or more of them is false.

5. Another useful truth-functional concept is <u>disjunction</u>, represented by the word "or" or by the words "Either...or....".
The statement "His hair was black or dark brown" is the disjunction of the statements "................." and "....................".

"His hair was black" ... "His hair was dark brown".

6. The disjunction "S or T" of two statements S and T is written "S v T". (The sign "v" is from the Latin word "vel".)
S v T is defined as a statement which is true when <u>either S is true or T is true or both</u>, and false when S and T are both false.

  If S is true and T false, S v T is ....
  If S is false and T true, S v T is ....
  If S and T are both true, S v T is ....

---

true (all cases).

7. The sign "v" is used to indicate what is called the <u>non-exclusive</u> sense of "or", as in "S or T <u>or both</u>". Sometimes, however, when we use the word "or", or the words "Either ....or", we intend them in the exclusive sense, as in "S or T <u>but not both</u>".
If an examination-paper carries the instruction "Candidates should attempt <u>either</u> Part A <u>or</u> Part B" this would normally be understood in the .... sense.

---

exclusive

8. If I were to return to an empty house and find the door open, and say "Either I left it open or there has been an intruder" my statement

would best be understood in the .... sense.

---

non-exclusive

9. It is not always clear which sense of "or" is intended. Strong emphasis on the word "or" usually (though not always) indicates the exclusive sense. The symbol "v", however, is <u>always</u> used to indicate the non-exclusive sense, "S or T <u>or both</u>".

If S and T are both true, S v T is ....
If S and T are both false, S v T is .....

---

true
false
(in that order)

10. The formula
$$S.T \longrightarrow S \lor T$$
means that "S and T" implies "S or T". Is this a valid implication?

Yes.

11. Let S mean "Ecuador is in South America" and let T mean "Ecuador is in Africa". In the sentence "Ecuador is in South America or Africa" the word "or" may be used indifferently in its exclusive or non-exclusive sense, since we <u>already know independently</u> that Ecuador cannot be in South America and Africa at the same time. Consequently we can symbolise this sentence simply in the non-exclusive form, namely as ....

S v T.

12. We can form disjunctions of three (or more) statements as in S v T v U, which can be interpreted as S v (T v U): the brackets are, however, unnecessary. Since "v" indicates the <u>non-exclusive</u> sense of "or" this means "At least one of S, T and U is true".

63

---

true.

13. When we use negation with disjunction, we must again be careful to use brackets to distinguish, say -(S v T) which means "It is not the case that either S or T is true" from -S v T which means "........................."

(In suitable words:)
"Either S is false or T is true (or both)".

14. Write in symbols "Either S is the case or T is not the case (or both)".
(In future we shall take "or both" for granted.)

S v -T

15. When conjunction and disjunction are used together, bracketing is often important. Thus the formula (S.T) v U means "Either S and T are true, or U is true"; whereas the formula S.(T v U) means "..................................."

(In suitable words:)
"S is true, and either T is true or U is".

16. The formula -(S.T) which says "It is not the case that S and T are both true", is false if and only if S and T are both true. That is to say, it is _true_ if and only if S is false, or T is false, or both. Consequently it is equivalent to the disjunction of -S and -T; that is, to ....

-S v -T.

17. We use the two-way arrow "⟷" to symbolise equivalence.

We have just proved as valid the equivalence

$$-(S.T) \longleftrightarrow -S \text{ v } -T.$$

Suppose we negate both sides of this equivalence relation. On the left-hand side the two negations cancel out. Consequently we can write the result as

$$S.T \longleftrightarrow \ldots\ldots\ldots$$

(Complete the formula)

-(-S v -T).

18. In the previous example we showed that conjunction can be expressed in terms of negation and disjunction. Now let us turn this result round, interchanging conjunction and disjunction. The disjunction S v T is <u>false</u> if and only if S and T are both false, and hence <u>true</u> if and only if S and T are <u>not</u> both false.

Write in symbols "The disjunction of S and T is equivalent to the negation of the conjunction of -S and -T".

S v T $\longleftrightarrow$ -(-S. -T)

19. Writing S for "There was petrol", T for "There was a spark" and U for "The engine started", write in symbols

"Either there was no petrol or there was no spark; and the engine did not start".

(-S v -T). -U
(<u>Note bracketing</u>)

20. If S and T are true and U is false, which of the following are true?

    (1) -S v T v -U ?
    (2) (-S v T). -U ?
    (3) (-S v T). U ?

(Write the number or numbers, or "None")

---

(1), (2)

21.   If S is true, S v T is true independently of whether T is. Consequently the implication   S⟶ S v T is valid.

Which of the following implications are valid?

    (1) -S⟶ -S v T ?
    (2) S.T⟶ S v T ?
    (3) S v -T⟶ S v T ?

(Write the number or numbers, or "None")

---

(1), (2)

22.   If we ever need to specify, in symbols, the <u>exclusive</u> disjunction "S or T but not both", we can do so directly by symbolising "S or T, and not both S and T", that is ....
(Write the formula)

(S v T). -(S. T)
(<u>N.B. Brackets essential</u>)

END OF CHAPTER 7

Chapter 8: Implication and Truth-Tables

In this chapter we consider some properties of the implication symbol " ⟶ " and introduce truth-tables as a method of checking for such properties.

1. When we write a formula such as S. T ⟶ S we use the sign " ⟶ " to indicate that the left-hand side <u>implies</u> the right-hand side: we can read the formula as "S-and-T <u>implies</u> S", or "<u>If</u> S and T (are true), <u>then</u> S (is true)".

In this case, the formula S. T ⟶ S is (true, false). (Which?)

---

true.

2. The formula S. T ⟶ S does not tell us anything about whether the left-hand side or right-hand side is actually true; but merely that if the one is true, <u>then</u> the other is true.

It is sometimes called a <u>conditional</u> or <u>hypothetical</u> statement. Which of the following are true?
(1) S. -T ⟶ -T ?
(2) S ⟶ S ?
(3) -(S. T) ⟶ -S v -T ?
(Write the number or numbers, or "None")

---

(1), (2), (3)

3. We use an arrow with a stroke through it, as "↛ ", to mean "does not imply".

Which of the following are true?

(1) S.T $\not\longrightarrow$ S ?
(2) S $\not\longrightarrow$ S ?
(3) S $\not\longrightarrow$ S.T ?
(Write the number or numbers, or "None")

---

4. If p and q are any two statements, "p $\longrightarrow$ q" means "p implies q" or "If p is true, so is q"; and "p $\not\longrightarrow$ q" means "p does not imply q" or "From the truth of p it does not follow that q is true too".

The formula "p $\longrightarrow$ -q" means "If p is true, q is false". Does this mean the same as "p $\not\longrightarrow$ q"?

No.

5. We have seen before that all the seven logical relations can be expressed in terms of implication. If p and q are any two statements, and the formulae "p $\longrightarrow$ q", "q $\not\longrightarrow$ p" are both true, what is the relation of p to q?

Superimplication.

6. Now suppose the formula "p $\longrightarrow$ -q", "-q $\not\longrightarrow$ p" are both true. The first says that if p is true q isn't; that is, p and q cannot both be true. The second says that if q is false, it does not follow that p is true; that is, p and q could conceivably both be false. It follows that the relation of p to q is ....

---

contrariety.

7. If the formulas "p $\longrightarrow$ -q", "-p $\longrightarrow$ q" are both true, what is the relation of p to q?

---

contradiction.

68

8. Let us suppose that p represents the statement "S. T" and q represents "S". Which of the following are true?

    (1) p ⟶ q ?
    (2) p ⟿ q ?

---

(1)

9. Could "p ⟶ q" and "p ⟿ q" ever <u>both</u> be true at the same time?

No.

10. If p represents "Jones and his girl friend did not both catch the bus" and q represents "Either Jones did not catch the bus or his girl friend didn't", which of the following is true?

    (1) p ⟶ q ?
    (2) q ⟶ p ?

(Write the number or numbers or "Neither")

---

(1), (2)

11. In the previous example, what is the logical relation of p to q?

Equivalence.

12. In which of the following cases, if any, is "p ⟶ q" true?
    (1) p represents "S v T", q represents "T"?
    (2) p and q both represent "-(S. T)"?
    (3) p represents "The dam is overflowing and the spillways are awash", and q represents "The dam is overflowing but the spillways are not awash"?

(Write the number or numbers, or "None")

---

(2)

13. Now let us look at some <u>general</u> properties of the implication sign " → ", that hold independently of the meanings of what we put for the letters on left- or right-hand side.

One such property is obvious from previous examples: if we put <u>the same</u> statement on the left- and right-hand sides, we always get a true statement.

That is, p → p is always true.

Which of the following are similarly always true?

    (1) p +→ p?
    (2) p → -p?

(Write the number or numbers, or "Neither")

Neither.

14. An important property of " → " is the property of being <u>transitive</u>, expressed in the so-called "chain rule":

If p → q and q → r are both true, then p → r is true.

As a simple application of the chain rule, for example, since

$$S.T.U → S.T$$
and S.T → T

are both true, it follows that . . . . is true. (Fill in the blank.)

S.T.U → T

15. A simpler, and more trivial, rule resembling the chain rule is the rule sometimes called the rule of "detachment" or "<u>modus ponens</u>" - the latter name is the traditional Latin one and means "affirming mode". The rule can be stated:

If p and p → q are both true, so is q.

In application we usually assume p to be simply a <u>true statement</u>, and p → q a statement of a <u>logical relation</u>. For example; If S.T is true, then, since S.T → S is true (i.e, is a valid implication), ... is true. (Fill in the blank.)

S

16. If p → q is true and q is <u>false</u>, p clearly cannot be true: it must be false also. This can be expressed by saying that, related to any

70

implication of the form "p ⟶ q" there is a <u>contraposed</u> (or <u>contra-positive</u>) implication of the form "-q ⟶ -p".

To contrapose an implication you must (1) interchange the two sides and (2) negate each side.

Consider the implication:

"Jones and Smith are both tall" implies "Jones is tall".

In contraposed form this would read:

"................." implies "..............."

"Jones is not tall" .... "Jones and Smith are not both tall". (N.B. order of sentences important).

17. It should be noticed carefully, however, that if we had <u>only</u> interchanged the two sides of the implication, or <u>only</u> negated them, we would not necessarily have reached a true formula.

Of the following "rules" some are valid and some not. Which are the valid ones?

(1) If p implies q and p is true, q is true.
(2) If p implies q and q is true, p is true.
(3) If p implies q and p is false, q is false.
(4) If p implies q and q is false, p is false.
(Write the numbers of the valid ones)

---

(1), (4)

18. Very often two or more statements combine together to imply another statement. We speak of such statements as <u>premisses</u> and the statement they imply as the <u>conclusion</u>.

We can set up various special rules for these cases. For example:
(1) Premisses may be taken in any order.
(2) Adding an <u>extra</u> premiss never invalidates a valid inference. (If p and q together imply s, then p, q and r together imply s).

However, we can always consider premisses as joined together by conjunction, "and", into a single one. That is, "p, q and r together imply s" can be written ....

---

p.q.r ⟶ s.

19.   Does "S" imply "S v T"?

The latter formula "S v T" is true whenever S is true, or T is true, or when both are.

Consequently, whenever S is true, "S v T" is true, and the answer to our question is "Yes".

What is the definition of "implies"?

A statement p <u>implies</u> another statement q if ....

(In suitable words:)

whenever p is true, q is true too.

20.   Here is a "truth-table" in which we can compare "S v T" with S. (Using "1" for "true" and "0" for "false":)

S	T	S v T
1	1	1
1	0	1
0	1	1
0	0	0

The four rows of the truth-table represent the four different possibilities of truth and falsehood of S and T. In the two cases in which S is true --namely, in the first two rows — S v T is true too. Hence, without looking at the other cases, we can say that S implies S v T.

From which rows can you deduce that T implies S v T?

The first and third.

21.   Does S. T imply S v T?

Here is a truth-table in which both S. T and S v T have been tabulated, for all the possible cases of truth or falsehood of S and T:

S	T	S. T	S v T
1	1	1	1
1	0	0	1
0	1	0	1
0	0	0	0

Because S.T is .... in row/rows no .... and S v T is ..... in the same row or rows, we see that S.T .... S v T.

Because S.T is true in row no. 1 and S v T is true in the same row, S.T does imply S v T.

22.   Here is a truth-table for (S.T) v U and S.(T v U). (For simplicity, only the result is given: the columns necessary for calculation are not shown).

S	T	U	(S.T) v U	S.(T v U)
1	1	1	1	1
1	1	0	1	1
1	0	1	1	1
1	0	0	0	0
0	1	1	1	0
0	1	0	0	0
0	0	1	1	0
0	0	0	0	0

Does either imply the other?

S.(T v U) implies (S.T) v U.

23.   Let us suppose that we know that p and q are truth-functions of, say, S and T, but that all we know about them is their truth-table, which is as follows:

S	T	p	q
1	1	0	0
1	0	0	1
0	1	1	1
0	0	0	0

Does either imply the other?   Does either of them imply S or T?

---

p implies q and p implies T.

24.   Calculate a truth-table for S.-T and -(S.T).

c*

73

S	T	S. -T	-(S. T)
1	1		
1	0		
0	1		
0	0		

S	T	S. -T	-(S. T)
1	1	0	0
1	0	1	1
0	1	0	1
0	0	0	1

25. In the previous example, does either statement imply the other? Does either imply S or T?

S. -T implies -(S. T)
S. -T implies S

26. Calculate a table for (S v T). -S and say whether it implies S or T. (Use intermediate columns for calculation as necessary).

S	T	S v T	-S	(S v T). -S
1	1			
1	0			
0	1			
0	0			

The column for (S v T). -S should read "0 - 0 - 1 - 0".
(S v T). -S implies T.

27. Returning to the simple example S. T ⟶ S, let us see how the contraposed form of the implication is shown to be valid by the "truth-table" method.

S	T	S. T
1	1	1
1	0	0
0	1	0
0	0	0

74

implication

To check the simple inference S. T $\nrightarrow$ S, we see that wherever S. T has 1, S has 1 also.

To check the contraposed form of the inference it would be enough to check that wherever S has 0, S. T has 0 also. Which rows of the table check this?

Rows 3 and 4.

28.   Draw up a table for -S and -(S. T) and say how it shows <u>directly</u> that -S implies -(S. T).

S	T	-(S. T)	-S
1	1	0	0
1	0	1	0
0	1	1	1
0	0	1	1

-S has 1 in rows 3 and 4, and in these rows so does -(S. T).

29.   The following is an alternative formulation of the condition that p implies q: There must be no row of the truth - table which gives p as true and at the same time q as false.

Try out the criterion on the following truth-table, where p and q are truth-functions of same pair of statements.

p	q
1	1
0	0
0	1
1	0

Which row, if any, invalidates "p $\longrightarrow$ q"?
Which row, if any, invalidates "q $\longrightarrow$ p"?

Row 4 invalidates p →q

p $\longrightarrow$ q is valid.   Row 3 invalidates q $\longrightarrow$ p.

30.   Two statements are equivalent if each implies the other. Suppose p and q are equivalent. This means that p is true whenever q is, and q is true whenever p is.   This is the same as saying that,

75

in every row of the truth-table, p has the same value as q.

Construct a truth-table for -(S. T) and -S v -T, and check that they are equivalent.

S	T	S. T	-(S. T)	-S	-T	-S v -T
1	1					
1	0					
0	1					
0	0					

The columns for -(S. T) and -S v -T should both read "0 - 1 - 1 - 1".

31.   In the following truth-table, p, q and r are truth-functions of some pair of statements.

p	q	r
0	1	1
1	1	0
0	0	1
1	1	1

We would say that p and q together imply r if, in every row in which p and q are both true, r is true also.

Do p and q together imply r? If not, why not?

No.   In the second row, p and q are true but r is not.

32.   In the previous example, which pair of statements implies the third?

---

p and r imply q.

END OF CHAPTER 8

The determination of logical relations from truth-tables is dealt with further in the optional chapter 12.

Chapter 9: Tautologies and Material Implication

Tautologies and their truth-tables are introduced, and material implication is used to provide a simple test for the existence of an implication relation.

1. In truth-functional logic — the logic we have been dealing with in the last three chapters — statements may be either simple or compound. The simple statements are those such as S, T and U which consist of a single letter. In our examples we normally assume that these stand for relatively simple statements such as "Jones is here" or "The grass is green".
Compound - statements are those formed out of simple statements using the truth-functional operators "-", ".", "v", and others that we shall introduce shortly.

If S and T are true and U is false, which of the following compounds are true?

(1) S. -T ?
(2) S v T v U ?
(3) -(S. T). -U ?
(Write the number or numbers, or "None")

---

(2)

2. We shall use the letters S, T, ... to denote simple statements; and, when we want to refer to compound statements without specifying just what compound they are, we shall call them p, q, ...
We assume the simple statements S, T. ... to be quite unrelated to one another. That is, the logical relation of S to T is ....

---

indifference.

3. Calculate a truth-table for (S. T) v (S. -T) and say what simple statement it is equivalent to.

S	T	S. T	-T	S. -T	(S. T) v (S. -T)
1	1				
1	0				
0	1				
0	0				

The final column reads "1 - 1 - 0 - 0" and this is the same as the column for S. Hence (S. T) v (S. -T) is equivalent to S.

4. Now let us consider some truth-functions that give special kinds of table.

By definition, -S cannot be true at the same time as S.

Consequently the conjunction S. -S will always have one conjunct false, and will always be false. It is a "self-contradiction".

Since it has only one component-statement S, a two-row table is sufficient to demonstrate this. Complete the following table:

S	-S	S. -S
1		
0		

S	-S	S. -S
1	0	0
0	1	0

5. Express the formula "(S v T). -S. -T" in words, and calculate a truth-table for it, in the form:

S	T	S v T	-S	(S v T). -S	-T	(S v T). -S. -T

(In suitable words:)
"Either S or T is true, and S is false, and T is false". The last column of the table has "0 - 0 - 0 - 0".

6. A self-contradiction can never be true, whatever the values of the component statements. It is also possible to construct statements that are always true. These are called <u>tautologies</u>. The simplest example is "S v -S" since one of the disjuncts must always be true.

Put the formula "(S. T) v -S v -T " in words, and calculate a truth-table for it similar to that in the last example.

(In suitable words:)
"Either S and T are true, or S is false, or T is false". The last column of the table has "1 - 1 - 1 - 1".

7. To reiterate:
Statements whose truth-table is a column of 1s are called . . . .
and statements whose truth-table is a column of 0s are called
. . . .

---

tautologies . . . . . . self-contradictions.

8. Most statements, which may sometimes be true and may sometimes be false, are neither tautologies nor self-contradictions.
They are said to be <u>contingent</u>.
A statement is <u>contingent</u> if its truth-table is a column which
. . . .

(In suitable words:)
. . . consists of a mixture of 1s and 0s.

9. A statement p is said to imply another statement q if, in a truth-table containing them, no row gives p as . . . . at the same time as it gives q as . . . . .

---

true . . . false
(in that order)

10. In the following truth-table, which of p, q and r implies which other?

79

p	q	r
0	1	1
1	0	0
1	0	1
0	1	1

---

q ──► r

11.   Up to the present, the statements in our examples of implication
have all been contingent.

Now suppose, say, q is a tautology: suppose, for example, p and q
have a truth-table as follows:

p	q
0	1
1	1
1	1
0	1

If we automatically apply the test for implication, what result do we
get?

It comes out that p implies q.

12.   In the previous example, it clearly would make no difference
<u>what</u> statement we put for p: there would still be no row with p true
and q false, <u>just because there could be no row with q false.</u>
From this we deduce that, according to the rule, a tautology is
implied by every other statement. (Even by a contradiction or another
tautology.)
Produce similar reasoning to show that, by the rule, a self-contradiction <u>implies</u> every other statement.

(In a suitable formulation:)
Whatever q is, if p is a self-contradiction then, you can never have p true
and q false, because p can never be true at all.

13.   For most purposes it is convenient to stick by the rule and
tolerate these so-called "paradoxes of implication". The reason

for this is mainly that this procedure makes our logic <u>simpler</u>; and makes no difference to practical cases where only <u>contingent</u> statements are involved.

We shall accept it as true, then, that a tautology .... any other statement, and a self - contradiction .... ¹any other statement.

---

is implied by ... implies
(<u>in that order</u>)

14. If p and q are both tautologies we shall have to say that each implies the other, and hence that they are <u>equivalent</u>.
Is the same true if p and q are both self-contradictions? Why?

Yes. A self-contradiction implies any other statement, and hence any two self-contradictions imply each other, and are equivalent.

15. Without calculating a truth - table in detail, say which of the statements S and T v -T implies the other, and why.

S implies T v -T, because T v -T is a tautology.

16. What implications hold between the following statements, and why?

(1) S. T
(2) S v -T
(3) S. -S

The first implies the second

The last implies each of the other two, because it is a self-contradiction.

17. What <u>equivalences</u> hold amongst the following statements, and why?

(1) S. -S
(2) S v -S
(3) T. -T

The first is equivalent to the third, since both are self-contradictions.

81

18. We are now in a position to introduce a concept which greatly simplifies the expression and derivation of implication relations. It is called "material implication" and the basic idea consists in the introduction of a new truth-functional sign. We shall write "S ⊃ T" ("S materially implies T") to mean "It is not the case that S is true and T false": that is , "-(S. -T)".

Calculate a truth-table for this formula.

Without intermediate working, the result is

S	T	-(S. -T)
1	1	1
1	0	0
0	1	1
0	0	1

19. Looking at the truth-table just calculated, we see that it has 1 in every row except the row in which S is true and T false.

Now consider two compound statements, p and q. If p is ever true at the same time as q is false, the formula "p ⊃ q" will have 0 in its truth table: otherwise it will have all 1s. That is to say that p implies q if and only if the formula "p ⊃ q" is a ....

---

tautology.

20. We can calculate a truth-table for p ⊃ q from the table for p and the table for q, row by row, by the following rules: p ⊃ q is false if p is true and q false; it is true if p is ..... or if q is ..... (Complete the rule)

---

false ..... true.
(in that order)

21. Is S. T ⊃ S a tautology?
Calculate a truth-table to check.

Yes.

S	T	S.T	S. T ⊃ S
1	1	1	1
1	0	0	1
0	1	0	1
0	0	0	1

22. We must remember that "S materially implies T", that is, "S ⊃ T", is really just a truth-function of S and T: it means "It is not the case that S is true and T false". Alternatively, it means "Either S is false, or T is true (or both)". Write the latter directly in symbols and show that its truth - table is the same as that for S ⊃ T.

-S v T

S	T	-S	-S v T
1	1	0	1
1	0	0	0
0	1	1	1
0	0	1	1

23. The statement "All squares are five-sided" is false, and the statement "Cairo is in Egypt" is true. Does the first materially imply the second?

Yes.

24. However, many of the properties of implication hold for material implication too: for example, <u>modus ponens</u> in the following form.

If p is true and p ⊃ q is a tautology , q is true
In fact, p ⊃ q does not need to be a tautology here: it is enough if it

is simply true. Show this by calculating a truth-table for S.(S ⊃ T) and T and showing that one implies the other.

S	T	S ⊃ T	S.(S ⊃ T)
1	1	1	1
1	0	0	0
0	1	1	0
0	0	1	0

S.(S ⊃ T) has 1 in the first row only, and here T has 1 too.

25.   We can express the fact that S.(S ⊃ T) implies T by saying that the formula (S.(S ⊃ T)) ⊃ T is a tautology.   (The brackets are necessary as shown.)
In the same way, if S ⊃ T is true and T is false, S must be false. What formula, to express this, must be a tautology?

((S ⊃ T).-T) ⊃ -S   or   (-T.(S ⊃ T)) ⊃ -S.

26.   The parallel between these formulae and implication relations is so close that it is usual amongst logicians to read the sign " ⊃ " simply as "implies" or "If... then... " and to say that formulae containing it express implication. (This way of speaking can lead to trouble, but when we are in doubt we may revert to the more careful way of putting things.)
    What formula, then, expresses the chain rule for material implication: namely that if S ⊃ T and T ⊃ U are both true, S ⊃ U is true?

((S ⊃ T).(T ⊃ U)) ⊃ (S ⊃ U)

27.   What formula expresses the fact that a tautology   (say, T v -T) is implied by any statement at all?

S ⊃ (T v -T)

28.   Is the contraposed form "-T ⊃ -S" of the material implication "S ⊃ T" equivalent to it? (Calculate a truth-table to find out.)

Yes.

S	T	S ⊃ T	-T	-S	-T ⊃ -S
1	1	1	0	0	1
1	0	0	1	0	0
0	1	1	0	1	1
0	0	1	1	1	1

END OF CHAPTER 9

Chapter 10: Material Equivalence: Rules of Inference

This chapter deals with some subsidiary questions that complete our elementary account of the logic of unanalysed statements.

    1.   If S and T are true and U is false, which of the following are true?
        (1) S ⊃ T ?
        (2) (S v T) ⊃ U ?
        (3) (S ⊃ T) ⊃ U ?
(Write the number or numbers, or "None")

---

(1)

    2.   A table which sets out the value (true or false) of a compound statement in terms of the simple statements composing it is called a . . . .

---

truth-table.

    3.   When a compound statement has the value 1 independently of the values of the simple statements in it, it is called a . . . .

---

tautology.

    4.   When the truth-table of a statement shows that it may have the value 1 and may have the value 0 , it is called . . . .

---

contingent.

5. The statement "S ⊃ T" is (a tautology, a self-contradiction, contingent). (Which?)

---

contingent.

6. Fill in the basic truth-table for the formula "S ⊃ T", as follows.

S	T	S ⊃ T
1	1	
1	0	
0	1	
0	0	

The column should read "1 - 0 - 1 - 1".

7. Fill in the following two-row truth-table for S ⊃ S, and say what it shows about this formula.

S	S ⊃ S
1	
0	

The column should read "1 - 1". The formula S ⊃ S is a tautology.

8. In the earlier part of this course we used the symbol " ➝ " to mean "implies". This was not, however, a truth-functional symbol, because the truth or falsehood of "p ➝ q" does not depend only on whether p and q are true, but also on how they are related.

For example, from the fact that "Roses are red" and "Violets are blue" are both true statements, you cannot deduce whether "Roses are red" implies "Violets are blue". (In this case, of course, it doesn't).

However, "material implication" is primarily a truth-function: "S ⊃ T" means "It is not the case that S is true and T false". Write this in terms of other truth-functional connectives "-" and ". ", or "-" and "v".

-(S. -T) or -S v T.

9. Does "Roses are red" <u>materially imply</u> "Violets are blue"? Why?

Yes. (In suitable words:)
Because both statements are true, and $S \supset T$ is true when both S and T are true.

10. If, for short, we read " $\supset$ " as simply "If ...... then" or "implies", the formula $((p \supset q) . p) \supset q$ can be read as "If p implies q, and p is true, then q is true". (Note that it is often convenient to use "If ... then ..." for the <u>main</u> connective, and "implies" for others.)

Put into words
$$((p \supset q) . -q) \supset -p$$

(Say:)
"If p implies q, and q is false, then p is false"

11. Put into words
$$(p \supset q) \supset ((q \supset r) \supset (p \supset r))$$

(Say:)
"If p implies q, then, if q implies r, p implies r"

12. Now suppose p and q imply one another. We would say that they are <u>equivalent</u>. In a n a l o g y with this we can say that "S is <u>materially equivalent</u> to T" will mean "S <u>materially implies</u> T and T <u>materially implies</u> S".

In symbols we write "$S \equiv T$" to mean "$(S \supset T) . (T \supset S)$".
Construct a truth-table for $S \equiv T$.

S	T	$S \supset T$	$T \supset S$	$(S \supset T) . (T \supset S)$
1	1			
1	0			
0	1			
0	0			

The column for $S \supset T$ reads "1 - 0 - 1 - 1".
The column for $T \supset S$ reads "1 - 1 - 0 - 1".
The column for $(S \supset T) . (T \supset S)$ reads "1 - 0 - 0 - 1".

13. We see from the table just calculated that S and T are <u>materially</u> <u>equivalent</u> when they are both true, or when they are both <u>false: that</u> is, when they <u>have the same value.</u>

Let S stand for "Spain is in Europe", T for "Coffee is made from tea-leaves" and U for "Three sevens are twenty-seven". From what you know of the truth of these statements, which is m a t e r i a l l y equivalent to which other?

T is materially equivalent to U.

14. We would say that two statements p and q were <u>equivalent,</u> in the strict sense of the word, if they <u>couldn't ever</u> have different values. This is the same as stipulating that the formula "p ≡ q" should be a <u>tautology.</u>

Construct a truth-table for the formula $(S.T) \equiv (T.S)$ and say how it shows that S.T is equivalent to T.S.

S	T	S.T	T.S	$(S.T) \equiv (T.S)$
1	1			
1	0			
0	1			
0	0			

The columns for S.T and T.S both read "1 - 0 - 0 - 0".
The column for $(S.T) \equiv (T.S)$, of course, reads "1 - 1 - 1 - 1", showing that this is a tautology.

15. Is $S.(S \supset T)$ equivalent to T?
Construct a truth-table to find out.

S	T	$S \supset T$	$S.(S \supset T)$	$(S.(S \supset T)) \equiv T.$
1	1	1	1	1
1	0	0	0	1
0	1	1	0	0
0	0	1	0	1

Since there is a 0 in the final column, they are not equivalent.

16.   To what simple formula is S.(S ⊃ T) equivalent? (Look at the column for S.(S ⊃ T) in the truth-table just calculated.)

S. T

17.   When two statements are equivalent they may be substituted one for another in any formula, without altering the truth or false-hood of that formula under any circumstances.
    We have just shown that S.(S ⊃ T) and S. T are equivalent.
What simpler formula is the rule of <u>modus ponens</u> (S.(S ⊃ T)) ⊃ T equivalent to?

(S. T) ⊃ T

18.   When S and T are both true, S ≡ T is true. Hence, if p and q are tautologies, and consequently always both true, "p ≡ q" is itself always true; that is, a tautology.
    If p and q are both self-contradictions, what can we deduce about p ≡ q?

It is a tautology.

END OF CHAPTER 10

    This completes the basic section of Part 2.
    Revision material for this section will be found in Revision Chapter 2.
    The following chapters 11 and 12 deal with certain special additional topics, which can be regarded as optional.

Chapter 11: Logic from Axioms

Previous chapters have treated the logic of unanalysed statements by the truth-table method; that is, truth-tables have been used as the test of whether one of two statements implies the other.

An alternative, more generally acceptable, procedure is to treat Logic as Geometry is treated: to set up axioms and deduce theorems from them.

This chapter outlines this alternative approach.

No part of the following chapters depends on this one, and it may be omitted or taken out of order.

1. Let us consider the <u>definitions</u> of the logical signs "−", ".", "v", " ⊃ " and "≡".

In previous chapter we have defined some of these in terms of others; for example, we defined

$$S \supset T \qquad =Df \qquad -(S.-T)$$

where the sign "=Df" means just "is defined as", or "is equal to, by definition".

Using this sign, write a corresponding definition of "≡"(i.e. write in symbols that "S ≡ T" is defined as "S materially implies T and T materially implies S").

$$S \equiv T \qquad =Df \qquad (S \supset T).(T \supset S)$$

2. When we introduced the sign for disjunction, "v", we remarked that "S or T or both" could alternatively be expressed "It is not the case that S and T are both false".

Hence write a definition of "S v T".

$$S \ v \ T \qquad =Df \qquad -(-S.-T)$$

3.   Alternatively, "S. T" could be regarded as defined similarly in terms of "–" and "v"; namely in the form "It is not the case that either S is false or T is false". Write the definition in symbols.

S. T   =Df   –(–S v –T)

4.   We cannot, however, **both** define "or" in terms of "and", **and** define "and" in terms of "or". Somewhere, that is, we must have an independent definition of one or the other.

In previous chapters we defined "and" and "not" independently in terms of truth and falsehood. For example, we said that "–S", the negation of S, is the statement which is

true when S is false, and
false when S is true.

Similarly, "S. T", the conjunction of S and T, was defined as the statement which is

true when ...., and
false when ....

.. S and T are both true
.. either S or T is false (or both).

5.   The definitions just given are equivalent to giving the truth-tables of the functions concerned.

Fill in the following truth-table definitions:

S	–S
1	
0	

S	T	S. T
1	1	
1	0	
0	1	
0	0	

The column for –S is "0 – 1".
The column for S. T is "1 – 0 – 0 – 0".

6.   However, by introducing truth-tables at the beginning, we took for granted certain things such as that every statement must be either true or false and no statement can be both at once. Logicians do not

always want to make these assumptions; and, even when they do, they prefer to know exactly what assumptions they are making.

Let us, then, take "−" and "v" as <u>elementary signs</u>, which we do not try to define; except that we shall set down some of their properties as axioms.

Having chosen (more or less arbitrarily) to start with "−" and "v", we define the others in terms of them.   Write definitions of ".", "⊃" and "≡" in terms of "−" and "v" directly.

S.T	=Df	-(-S v -T)
S⊃T	=Df	-S v T
S≡T	=Df	(-S v T).(-T v S)

7.   Before we decide on the most suitable set of axioms, let us consider some formulae we <u>might</u> put down.

Properties of "v" and "." that seem to be "axiomatic" are the "commutation rules":
$$(p \text{ v } q) \equiv (q \text{ v } p)$$
$$(p.q) \equiv (q.p)$$
We can put whatever formulae we like for p and q in rules of this kind.   For example, if we put -S for p and -T for q in the first one, we get the valid equivalence
$$(-S \text{ v } -T) \equiv (-T \text{ v } -S).$$
What do we get if we put S v T for p and U for q in the same formula? (Be careful about bracketing.)

$$((S \text{ v } T) \text{ v } U) \equiv (U \text{ v } (S \text{ v } T))$$

8.   A rule that we might rely on to deduce formulae from axioms is the following: When two formulae are equivalent, we may substitute one for the other wherever we wish.

Taking the result
$$((S \text{ v } T) \text{ v } U) \equiv (U \text{ v } (S \text{ v } T))$$
of the last example, what do we get if we substitute in accordance with the equivalence
$$(T \text{ v } S) \equiv (S \text{ v } T)$$
on the left-hand side only?

$$((T \text{ v } S) \text{ v } U) \equiv (U \text{ v } (S \text{ v } T))$$

93

9.   Another property that we might want as an axiom would be the "rule of double negation"

$$--p \equiv p.$$

Since this holds for any statement p, it will hold if we put -p for p, getting the new rule

$$---p \equiv -p.$$

Shall we be able to prove

$$----p \equiv p?$$

How?

By putting -p for p again, we get $----p \equiv --p$
and we can substitute --p for p because we already know $--p \equiv p.$

10.   Other properties what we might think of including are the "contraposition rule"

$$(p \supset q) \equiv (-q \supset -p)$$

and some rules for equivalence itself, such as

$$(p \equiv q) \equiv (-p \equiv -q).$$

However, some of these rules can easily be derived from some of the others.
Remembering that " $\equiv$ "is defined

$$p \equiv q \quad =Df \quad ((p \supset q).(q \supset p)$$

can you derive the above "equivalence" rule from the "contraposition" one?   How?

(In a suitable formulation:)
Since $p \equiv q$ is the same as $(p \supset q).(q \supset p)$ it is the same as $(-q \supset -p).(-p \supset -q)$ which, changing the order of the conjunctions, is the same as $-p \equiv -q.$

11.   For some purposes, all that matters is that we should put down clearly whatever rules we take to be self-evident.
It is natural, however, to see what is the least we can make do with in the way of axioms and rules.
    We shall distinguish formal axioms from rules of inference. Formal axioms are formulae that we may take for granted (as it were) as tautologies.   Rules of inference enable us to deduce new tautologies from the formal axioms.

94

As formal axioms it is sufficient to take the four formulae
1. $(p \lor p) \supset p$
2. $q \supset (p \lor q)$
3. $(p \lor q) \supset (q \lor p)$
4. $(q \supset r) \supset ((p \lor q) \supset (p \lor r))$

Express the last of these in words.

(Say:)
"If q implies r, then p-or-q implies p-or-r".

12.   Amongst the fundamental rules of inference we do not include the "substitution of equivalents" rule mentioned above. Instead, we use only the following two rules:

1.   (Substitution rule:) Given any tautology, substitution of any formula for any letter, throughout, will yield another tautology.

2.   (Rule of detachment or <u>modus ponens</u>:) Given two tautologies of the form f_1 and $f_1 \supset f_2$ respectively, where f_1 and f_2 are any formulae, we may deduce that f_2 is a tautology.

We have already had examples of the operation of the substitution rule. As an example of the operation of the rule of detachment, let us suppose that we have proved that

$$p \lor -p$$
and $(p \lor -p) \supset (q \lor p \lor -p)$

are tautologies. What follows?

---

q ∨ p ∨ -p is a tautology.

13.   Now let us prove some specimen "theorems"; that is, find ways of deriving new tautologies from the axioms given.

For example, we can prove the formula

$$(p \supset -p) \supset -p$$

from axiom 1. Axiom 1. is

$$(p \lor p) \supset p.$$

Substituting -p for p, we get

$$(-p \lor -p) \supset -p.$$

But, by the definition $p \supset q =Df -p \lor q$
we can substitute $p \supset -p$ for $-p \lor -p$.

95

This gives us the desired result.
Similarly deduce

$$q \supset (p \supset q)$$

from axiom 2.

Axiom 2. is $\quad q \supset (p \vee q)$.
Substituting -p for p we get $q \supset (-p \vee q)$.
By definition of "$p \supset q$" we get $q \supset (p \supset q)$.

14.   Here is an example of a rather longer deduction, leading to the simple tautology $p \supset p$.
We start with axiom 4., putting -p for p, p for r and p v p for q, getting:

$$((p \vee p) \supset p) \supset [(-p \vee (p \vee p)) \supset (-p \vee p)].$$

But from axiom 1. we have $(p \vee p) \supset p$. Hence by the rule of detachment

$$(-p \vee (p \vee p)) \supset (-p \vee p).$$

By the definition of material implication this becomes:

$$(p \supset (p \vee p)) \supset (p \supset p).$$

But from axiom 2., putting p for q, we have

$$p \supset (p \vee p).$$

Hence by the rule of detachment again:

$$p \supset p,$$

which is what we set out to prove.
Use this result and axiom 3. to prove

$$p \vee -p.$$

From axiom 3. by substitution of -p for p and p for q:

$$(-p \vee p) \supset (p \vee -p).$$

But from $p \supset p$ by definition of material implication:

$$-p \vee p.$$

Hence by detachment:

$$p \vee -p.$$

15.   It can be proved -- though it is beyond the scope of this course -- that every formula that comes out as a tautology by the truth-table test can also be proved from these axioms and rules; and vice versa.

The axioms and rules, however, only give us a method of finding tautologies. We must consider how we discover other properties of logical formulae.

96

A <u>self - contradiction</u> might be defined as a statement whose negation is a tautology. Hence, how would we show, from the axioms and rules, that a given statement was a self-contradiction?

By constructing a proof of its negation.

16. Let f_1 and f_2 be two formulae. How might we show, from the the axioms and rules, that f_1 <u>implies</u> f_2?

By constructing a proof of the formula $f_1 \supset f_2$.

17. Let us consider the question: How might we show that a given statement was <u>not</u> a tautology?

Since proofs can become quite complicated, the fact that we could <u>not</u> find a proof of the formula might mean nothing. Of course, if the statement happened to be a self - contradiction we might succeed in proving its negation. But, in general, we need another method.

The answer is connected with the general proof just mentioned; namely, the proof that the formulae provable from the axioms and rules are just those that come out as tautologies by the truth-table test, always having the value 1. <u>Given this proof</u>, we can use the truth-table test, knowing it to be equivalent to the axioms-and-rules test: a formula which does <u>not</u> always have the value 1 <u>cannot</u> be proved.

If we have a general method of proving a given formula <u>not</u> to be a tautology, how might we go on to prove it to be actually contingent?

By also proving that its negation is not a tautology, so that it is neither a tautology nor a self-contradiction.

<u>END OF CHAPTER 11</u>

Chapter 12: Logical Relations by Truth-Table

This optional chapter is concerned with the determination of logical relations between truth-functional formulae, and with the question of what logical relations hold when one or both of the statements is a tautology or a self-contradiction.

1. We have already had examples of a number of cases of logical relations between truth-functional statements.

The simplest case is that of implication.

We say that a statement p _implies_ another statement q if the formula p ⊃ q is . . . .

---

a tautology.

2. In the previous example, it is essential that p ⊃ q be a <u>tautology</u>, not merely <u>true</u>.

If S is "Grass is green" and T is "Copper conducts electricity", both statements being true, is S ⊃ T true?

Is it a tautology?

Yes.
No.
(<u>in that order</u>)

3. We shall use "p ⟶ q", as before, to mean "p ⊃ q is a tautology". Equivalently, this means "It is impossible for p to be . . . . at the same time as q is . . . . . ."

true
false.
(<u>in that order</u>)

4.   Using negation, we can write "p and q can't both be true" in the form

$$p \longrightarrow -q$$

Similarly, express in symbols "p and q can't both be false."

-p ⟶ q
(or -q ⟶ p.)

5.   Subject to a qualification to be mentioned later, we can express all the logical relations in this form.
The relation of p to q is <u>superimplication</u> if

$$p \longrightarrow q$$

$$q \not\longrightarrow p$$

The relation of p to q is <u>subimplication</u> if ... (Write the appropriate pair of formulae)

---

p ⟶̸ q
q ⟶ p
(<u>in either order</u>)

6.   The relation of p to q is <u>contrariety</u> if .... (Write the pair of formulae.

---

p ⟶ -q
-p ⟶̸ q
(<u>in either order</u>)

7.   The relation of p to q is <u>subcontrariety</u> if ...

---

p ⟶̸ -q
-p ⟶ q

8.   The relation of p to q is <u>contradiction</u> if ...

---

p ⟶ -q
-p ⟶ q

9.   The relation of p to q is <u>equivalence</u> if ...

---

p⟶q
q⟶p

10.   For the case of <u>indifference</u> we need to specify that none of the other relations apply.   Strictly speaking we need <u>four</u> formulae for this, namely

$$p \nrightarrow q \qquad\qquad q \nrightarrow p$$
$$p \nrightarrow -q \qquad\qquad -p \nrightarrow q$$

The formula q $\nrightarrow$ p is out of line with the others, since it has q on the left-hand side and p on the right: the others all have the reverse.

Using the rule of contraposition, how can we write an equivalent formula with p on the left and q on the right?

-p $\nrightarrow$ -q

11.   Hence the question of the logical relation of p to q can be reduced to the four questions:

   (1)   Whether p implies q,
   (2)   Whether p implies -q,
   (3)   Whether -p implies q and
   (4)   Whether -p implies -q.

Another way of putting these questions is in terms of possibilities of joint truth and falsehood of p and q: thus

   (a)   Is it possible to have p true and q false ?
   (b)   Is it possible to have p and q both true ?
   (c)   Is it possible to have p and q both false ?
   (d)   Is it possible to have p false and q true ?

Do the questions (a) — (d) correspond exactly, respectively, to the questions (1) — (4).   (Otherwise say in what respect they do not.)

They correspond, except that a "Yes" answer to (1) is equivalent to a "No" answer to (a), and so on.

12.   Given the four conditions on p and q:

100

     (i) p.q   impossible,
    (ii) p.-q possible,
   (iii) -p.q possible,
   (iv) -p.-q impossible.

What is the relation of p to q ?

Contradiction.

13.   Given the four conditions:

    (i) p $\not\rightarrow$ q
   (ii) p $\not\rightarrow$ -q
  (iii) -p $\rightarrow$ q
  (iv) -p $\not\rightarrow$ -q

What is the relation of p to q ?

Subcontrariety.

14.   Now let us consider the complication referred to above. Let q be a tautology; for example, let it stand for S $\supset$ S.

Now q cannot be false, and so, by our rule, since it is impossible to have p true and q false, p <u>must imply</u> q, quite independently of what p is.

Every statement, as we said, implies a tautology.

Which of the following four c o n d i t i o n s must hold if q is a tautology ?

   (1) p $\rightarrow$ q   ?
   (2) p $\rightarrow$ -q ?
   (3) -p $\rightarrow$ q ?
   (4) -p $\rightarrow$ -q ?

(Write the number or numbers)

---

(1), (3).

15.   Let p be the statement "Roses are red" and let q be the statement "Either it is raining or it isn't". We would not normally say that there is any logical relation between these statements.

However, since q is a tautology, we feel compelled to say that p implies q, and also that -p implies q.

Now suppose, alternatively, that p is a self-contradiction and that q is contingent. Which of the following four conditions holds?

(1) p ⟶ q   ?
(2) p ⟶ -q   ?
(3) -p ⟶ q   ?
(4) -p ⟶ -q ?

(Write the number or numbers)

---

(1), (2)

16.   If p were a self-contradiction <u>and</u> q were a tautology, which of the four conditions in the previous example would apply?

---

(1), (2), (3)

17.   Our dilemma is a common one in Logic — or, generally, in Philosophy —: we have a rule which leads to consequences we do not want to accept.

The solution in the present case is to qualify the rule. Let us simply say that the classical theory of the seven logical relations applies <u>only to contingent statements</u>.

Thus, if "p ⟶ q" is a valid formula and p and q are <u>both contingent</u>, the relation must be superimplication or equivalence; but if either p or q is a tautology or a self-contradiction we shall say that, at least in the classical sense, neither of these relations applies.

A statement is <u>contingent</u> if it is neither a .... nor a....
....

---

tautology
self-contradiction
(in that order)

18.   If a statement is a tautology, its truth-table is all 1s.

102

If it is a self-contradiction, its truth-table is .....

If it is contingent, its truth-table is .....

---

all 0s
a mixture of 1s and 0s.
(in that order)

   19.   The following is a section of a truth-table giving p, q and r as truth-functions of some statements.
   Between which pair of statements does one of the classical seven logical relations hold, and what is it?

p	q	r
1	1	1
1	1	1
1	1	1
0	1	0

---

p and r: Equivalence.

   20.   Between which pair of p, q, r does one of the classical seven relations hold in the following case, and what is it?

p	q	r
0	0	0
0	0	0
0	0	1
0	1	1

---

q and r: Superimplication
(or r and q: Subimplication)

   21.   What is the relation between two contingent statements p and q if there is no row of the truth-table in which they both have 1, but there is a row in which they both have 0?

Contrariety.

103

22. What is the relation of p to q in the following case?

p	q
0	1
1	0
0	1
1	0

Contradiction.

23. What is the relation of p to q in the following case?

p	q
1	0
0	1
1	1
0	0

Indifference.

24. Now let us illustrate that the answers to the four questions

    (1) Is it possible to have p and q both true ?
    (2) Is it possible to have p true and q false ?
    (3) Is it possible to have p false and q true ?
    (4) Is it possible to have p and q both false ?

not only give us the logical relation of p to q, if there is one, but also tell us whether p and q are both contingent and, if they are not, whether they are tautologies or self-contradictions.

Let us suppose, for example, that we get the answer "No" to (1) and (2), and "Yes" to (3) and (4).

Since, from the answer "No" to (1) and (2), p and q can't both be true, and we also can't have p true and q false, p can't be true at all, and must be a self-contradiction. However, q can be true and can be false, by the "Yes" answers to (3) and (4), so that it is contingent.

Perform a similar reasoning process for the case in which (1) and (3) have "No" answers, and (2) and (4) have "Yes".

Since (1) and (3) have "No", q is a self-contradiction.
Since (2) and (4) have "Yes", p is contingent.

25.   Now suppose we have the answer "No" to questions (1), (2) and (3).   The answer "No" to (1) and (2) implies that p is a self-contradiction.   The answer "No" to (1) and (3) implies that q is a self-contradiction.

In effect, since (4) is the only question getting a "Yes" answer, the joint falsehood of p and q is the only possibility.

Other cases can be worked out similarly.

A final question: Could we have a "No" answer to <u>all four</u> questions?

A "No" answer to (1) and (2) implies that p is a self-contradiction.

A "No" answer to (3) and (4) implies that p is a tautology.
Is there any sense in saying that something is a tautology and a self-contradiction at the same time?

No.

END OF CHAPTER 12

END OF PART 2

(Table of possible logical relations is given on page 182.)

Part 3
The Logic of Predicates

Part 2 dealt with the logic of statements treated as unanalysed wholes, except in so far as they could be treated as conjunctions, disjunctions, etc. of other statements.

In this Part we turn our attention to kinds of inference in which it is necessary to analyse the statements into, say, subject and predicate. This leads to a considerably wider field of applications.

Chapter 13: Syllogisms

Logicians since Aristotle have studied inferences such as "All men are mortal; all Greeks are men; therefore, all Greeks are mortal." An inference of this sort is called a syllogism.

In this chapter a sketch of the traditional theory of syllogisms is given, leading up to their treatment in modern terms. Knowledge of the material in Part 1, including chapter 5, is assumed. Later chapters will also assume knowledge of Part 2, chapters 6 - 10.

1. The Logic to be dealt with in this chapter is concerned with statements of the four forms:

All As are Bs
No As are Bs
At least one A is a B
At least one A is not a B.

(It used, at one time, to be held by logicians that all statements were of these forms.)

In Part 1 we dealt with the traditional arrangement of statements of this kind in the corners of a square. For example:

106

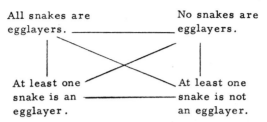

All snakes are egglayers. ———————— No snakes are egglayers.

At least one snake is an egglayer. ———————— At least one snake is not an egglayer.

Let us revise the properties of this square. (Assume for the moment, that empty terms do not occur.)

The square is arranged on the principle that the relation across the diagonals, e.g. between "All snakes are egglayers" and "At least one snake is not an egglayer", is ....

---

contradiction.

2. On the other hand, the relation between "All snakes are egg-layers" and "No snakes are egglayers" -- that is, across the top of the square -- is ....

---

contrariety.

3. And the relation down the sides of the square -- e.g. of "All snakes are egglayers" to "At least one snake is an egglayer" -- is ....

---

superimplication.

4. Two statements are said to be c o n t r a r i e s when they can't .... but can ....

---

both be true
both be false.
(in that order)

5. One statement is said to imply another when it is impossible for

107

the first to be .... at the same time as the second is .....

---

true
false.
(in that order)

    6.   On the other hand, if empty terms may occur, the easiest way to interpret "All As are Bs" is as meaning
               "There are no As that are not Bs"
which is automatically true if there are no As.
In this case, "All As are Bs" and "No As are Bs" can both be true, and are not contraries but ....

---

indifferent.

    7.   Similarly "All As are Bs" could be true when "At least one A is a B" is false, and consequently the relation (of the first to the second) is not superimplication but ....

---

indifference.

    8.   For the rest of this chapter we shall assume that empty terms **may** occur, and that, for example, "All As are Bs" and "No As are Bs" are indifferent. One way of thinking about a statement such as "All snakes are egglayers" is that it is a statement which says something about members of the class "snakes" and members of the class "egglayers". Strictly, there are <u>four</u> possible classes of things we might be interested in, namely

                (1) egglaying snakes
                (2) non-egglaying snakes
                (3) egglaying non-snakes
                (4) non-egglaying non-snakes.

Everything in the universe must belong to one or other of these classes. (Most things, of course, belong to class (4)).
    The statement "All snakes are egglayers", however, says that

there is <u>nothing at all</u> in a certain one of these classes. Which?
(Write the number)

---

(2)

9. Similarly, the statement "No snakes are egglayers" says that there is nothing at all in a certain one of the classes. Which? (Write the number)

---

(1)

10. Let us represent these facts pictorially, in a diagram.
Let us suppose that points inside the left hand circle represent "snakes" and points inside the

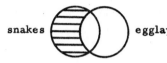
snakes ⬡ egglayers

right-hand circle "egglayers". Points in the region of overlap then represent "egglaying snakes", and so on.
Shading represents "emptiness": the shading of the left-hand section of the left-hand circle indicates that this region -- the region of "non-egglaying snakes" -- is empty. Hence what statement does the shading represent?

All snakes are egglayers.

11. Which of the regions in the diagram -- they have been labelled (1), (2), (3) for convenience -- would we shade to represent the statement "No pigs fly"?

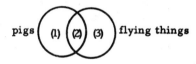
pigs (1) (2) (3) flying things

---

(2)

12. What kind of things are represented by region (3) in the diagram?

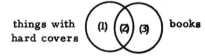
things with hard covers (1) (2) (3) books

109

Books without hard covers.

13. In the d i a g r a m the region <u>outside both</u> circles -- which we do not usually need to bother about -- has been shaded. What kinds of thing (would you say?) are represented by this region, and w h a t statement d o e s the shading represent?

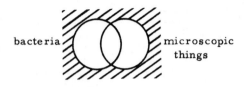
bacteria   microscopic things

Non-microscopic non-bacteria.
(Something like:) "Everything that isn't a bacterium is microscopic".

14. Which a r e a o f t h e figure would you shade to represent t h e statement "All band instruments are made of brass"? (Write the number)

things made of brass band instruments

---

(3)

15. To contradict a statement that a given class is <u>empty</u> it is necessary t o assert that it is <u>non-empty</u>; that is, that it has at least one member.

mammals swimming things

The diagram represents the statement "At least one mammal swims" because it has a stroke in the region r e p r e s e n t i n g the class "..............."

"swimming mammals".

16. It is traditional to use the word "Some" to mean "At least one", and we shall do so, for convenience, for the rest of this chapter.
Draw and mark a diagram to represent

110

"Some fish have ears"

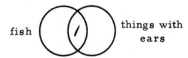

17. Draw and mark a diagram to represent the statement "Not all graduates are lecturers".

18. Draw and mark a diagram to represent the statement "All goobles are windomes".

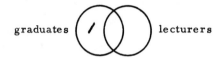

19. We can represent more than one statement on a single diagram. For example this diagram represents both "All ticket-holders are admitted" (horizontal shading)

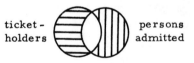

and "All those admitted are ticket-holders" (vertical shading)

The shading on this diagram represents the statement "All fish swim". Mark on it also the statement "Not everything that swims is a fish".

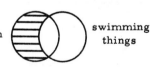

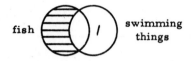

fish / swimming things

20. Shading of a region indicates that it is <u>empty</u>; a stroke in a region indicates that it is <u>non-empty</u>. If there is no mark at all in a region there is no indication whether it is empty or not.

An important point to note is that it is not permissible to have <u>shading</u> and <u>stroke</u> in the same region: this would indicate that the region is both empty and non-empty at the same time.

The statement "All drugs are habit - forming" and "Not all drugs are habit - forming" involve both shading and a stroke in region No. . . . . of this

drugs (1) (2) (3) habit-forming things

diagram, and this represents the fact that the statements are . . . .

---

(1)
contradictories (<u>or</u> inconsistent).

21. This diagram represents both the statement "All non-conducting metals are brittle" (horizontal s h a d i n g) and the statement "No non-conducting metal is brittle" (vertical shading).

non-conducting metals

brittle things

The fact that <u>the whole</u> of the left-hand circle has thus been shaded indicates that if the two statements are both true the term "non-conducting metal" must be . . . .

---

empty or vacuous.

22. The previous example shows us how we may use a diagram to <u>draw a conclusion</u> from two separate statements.

To apply this to syllogisms we need to deal with diagrams representing three terms: that is, with three overlapping circles.

In this diagram the region marked "(1)" represents "long complicated problems". What does the region "(2)" represent?

long things

complicated things

problems

"long problems that are not complicated".

23. In this diagram one of the starred ("*") regions represents "large powerful cars" and the other represents "large non-powerful cars"; so that the two together simply represent "large cars" (i.e. powerful or not). Taking the two regions marked "(a)" together, what class of things is represented?

powerful things

large things

cars

"non-large cars".

24. To mark a two-term statement (such as "All As are Bs") on a three-circle diagram we shall have to mark two adjoining regions together. Mark the diagram to represent "All men are mortal".

Greeks

men

mortals

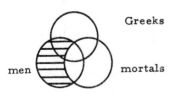

Greeks

men   mortals

113

25. Mark the following diagram to represent
"No doctors are dentists"

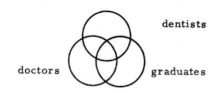

dentists

doctors   graduates

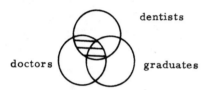

dentists

doctors   graduates

26. This diagram has been marked
to represent "All men are mortal"
(horizontal shading) and "All Greeks
are men" (vertical shading).

men

Now consider the region heavily outlined, namely, the part of the circle
for "Greeks" that lies outside the
circle for "mortals".

Greeks   mortals

This has all been shaded; partly as a result of representing the first
statement and partly as a result of representing the second. What
statement does the shading of this region represent?

"All Greeks are mortal".

27. A syllogism is an argument from two two-term statements to a
third: the two terms in the conclusion come one from each of the
premisses.
The previous example, in effect, was an example of a syllogism.

114

Here is another:

(Premisses) { No good teamsters are temperamental
All Olympic athletes are good teamsters.
(Conclusion) No Olympic athletes are temperamental.

Mark the two premisses on this diagram and outline the region that indicates the conclusion.

Olympic athletes

good teamsters

temperamental persons

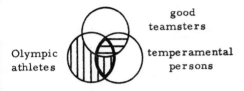

Olympic athletes

good teamsters

temperamental persons

28. Syllogisms, however, are not always valid. Consider the following example:

(Premisses) { All criminals are psychopaths
No scientists are criminals
(Conclusion) No scientists are psychopaths

By simple inspection this can be seen to be invalid; that is, the conclusion does not really follow from the premisses.
Put in your own words the reason the conclusion does not follow.

(In suitable words:)
From the fact that all criminals are psychopaths it doesn't follow that everyone who isn't a criminal isn't a psychopath. Hence some scientists could be psychopaths even if they are not criminals.

29. Draw and mark a diagram for the syllogism in the previous example, outlining the region that <u>should</u> be shaded if the conclusion were valid.

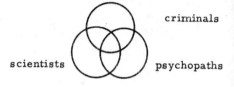

criminals

scientists

psychopaths

criminals

scientists

psychopaths

30. When one of the premisses involves shading and the other involves a stroke, the shading should be put in first. Consider the example

(Premisses) { All doctors are university graduates.
Some hospital employees are not university graduates

(Conclusion) Some hospital employees are not doctors.

If we had not put the shading in first, we would not have known which of the two starred regions to put the stroke in: as it is, only one of them is possible, consistently with the shading. Outline the region that should have a stroke in it in order that the conclusion should be valid. Has it a stroke in it?

university graduates

hospital employees

doctors

university graduates

hospital employees

doctors

Yes, the region outlined has a stroke in it.

116

31. Following the principle of the previous example, mark the premisses of the following (valid) syllogism on the diagram given, and outline the region referred to by the conclusion.

inert gases

radioactive substances

substances which form chemical compounds

(Premisses) { No inert gases form chemical compounds
Some inert gases are radioactive

(Conclusion) Some radioactive substances do not form chemical compounds

---

inert gases

radioactive substances

substances which form chemical compounds

32. In the case of an invalid syllogism involving a stroke, the invalidity shows up in the fact that we are unsure where to place the stroke.

university graduates

lawyers

dishonest persons

For example, in the syllogism

(Premisses) { All lawyers are university graduates
Some university graduates are dishonest

(Conclusion) Some lawyers are dishonest

-- after the first premiss has been shaded in as shown we do not know which of the two starred regions to put the stroke for the second premiss in.

Say in your own words why this syllogism is invalid.

(In suitable words:)
Although some university graduates may be dishonest it is possible that these ones are all non-lawyers, and that all lawyers are honest.

END OF CHAPTER 13

Chapter 14: Existential Presuppositions

This chapter, which may be omitted without upsetting the continuity of the course, deals with the fuller theory of syllogisms which allows for the possibility that some terms may be assumed non-empty.

1.   In the previous chapter we restricted ourselves, in the main, to the logic of statements whose terms were assumed to be <u>possibly</u> empty.

Thus to mark the diagram to represent "All unicorns are four-footed" we interpret this as meaning "There are no non-four-footed unicorns" and shade region (1) of the diagram.

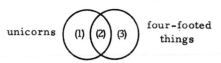

Similarly, to mark in "No unicorns are four-footed" we shade region (2).

But this involves shading <u>the whole</u> of the left-hand circle. What simple statement does the shading of this whole circle represent?

"There are no unicorns."

2.   We would normally regard two statements such as, say,
"All bachelors are happy"
and "No bachelors are happy"
as incompatible: that is, we would say that the relation between them was . . . .

---

contrariety.

3. But if "All As are Bs" and "No As are Bs" are contraries, there must be something wrong with the assumption that it is possible to shade a <u>whole</u> circle on our diagrams. That is, it must be assumed -- in most ordinary cases -- that the terms used are <u>non-empty</u>.

How do we indicate, on a diagram, that a given simple region is non-empty?

By putting a stroke in it.

4. In the previous chapter we sometimes found that we wanted to put a stroke in one of two adjoining regions, but were not sure which. Suppose that we are given a diagram as this and wish to express the statement "There exists at least one bachelor", without, for the moment, committing ourselves to whether bachelors are happy.

We want to indicate that there is <u>something</u> in the class indicated by the left-hand circle: whether in the region (1) or the region (2) or both. We have not so far provided any way of indicating this fact; but can do so by putting in a stroke which lies across the line, in this diagram.

This stroke will be taken to mean "There is at least one bachelor" - or, for short, "There are bachelors". In the same way, mark the diagram to indicate also "There are happy persons".

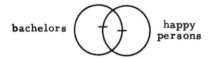

5. Now if a stroke runs across the boundary between the regions and we also s h a d e <u>one</u> of the regions, is there any inconsistency? What, in effect, happens to the stroke?

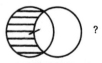

120

No, there is no contradiction. The stroke can be regarded as now lying wholly in the region not shaded.

6. The inference

(Premisses) $\begin{cases} \text{All bachelors are happy} \\ \text{There are bachelors} \end{cases}$
(Conclusion) Some bachelors are happy

can be regarded as a new kind of syllogism, involving only two terms.
Mark the premisses in on the diagram and outline the region involved by the conclusion. Is it valid?

bachelors happy persons

---

bachelors happy persons

Yes, it is valid.

7. Do the same for the "syllogism"

(Premisses) $\begin{cases} \text{No bachelors are happy} \\ \text{There are bachelors} \end{cases}$
(Conclusion) Some bachelors are not happy.

bachelors happy persons

---

bachelors happy persons

Valid.

8.   We shall call a statement like "There are bachelors" an <u>existential</u> statement (because it specifies the "existence" of bachelors).
We have seen that existential statements are often <u>taken for granted</u>, rather than being expressed explicitly.

What existential statement is being taken for granted when "All mammals are warm-blooded" is said to imply "At least one mammal is warm-blooded"?

"There are mammals"
(<u>or</u> "There is at least one mammal")

9.   What existential statement would be taken for granted by someone who said "All non-participants sat outside the ring: therefore there were some non-participants sitting outside the ring"?

"There are (or were) non-participants".

10.   We usually assume any terms we use to be not only <u>non-empty</u>, but also what we might call "non-full"; that is, we assume that there exist things to which the term does <u>not</u> apply. (When we use the term "physical object" we assume not merely that there are physical objects but also that there are things, whatever they are, that are <u>not</u> physical objects.

Can you think how to mark the statement "There are non-bachelors" on this diagram?   bachelors 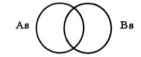 happy persons

---

bachelors 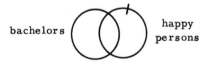 happy persons

11.   Mark this diagram to indicate that the terms "A" and "B" are both non-empty and "non-full"; that is that there are As, there are non-As, there are Bs and there are non-Bs.   As ◯◯ Bs

As ⊕ Bs

12. In a three-circle diagram a stroke indicating an
existential statement will
have to run through four
regions.
Mark 'There are scientists"
on this diagram.

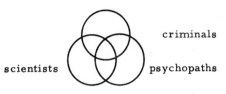

criminals

scientists

psychopaths

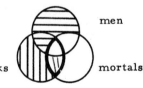

criminals

scientists   psychopaths

(or any other stroke that runs through the four regions concerned.)

13. The syllogism

(Premisses) {All men are mortal
{All Greeks are men
(Conclusion) Some Greeks are mortal

is shown as invalid by this diagram
since the region indicated by the
conclusion does not contain a stroke.
Putting in a stroke to indicate "an
extra premiss "There are Greeks",
however, would make it valid since
the only part of the stroke not shaded
out would be wholly in the outlined
region.
Would "There are men" do just as well?
Would "There are mortals" do?

men

Greeks   mortals

123

No. In both cases the stroke would lie partly outside the outlined region.

14. The syllogism

(Premisses) { No claustrophobes are speleologists
All speleologists are adventure-seekers.

(Conclusion) Some adventure-seekers are not claustrophobes.

-- is shown as invalid by this diagram.
Mark in as an additional premiss "There are speleologists", and say whether it makes it valid.

speleologists

adventure-seekers

claustrophobes

speleologists

adventure-seekers

claustrophobes

Yes: valid.
(The shaded-out part of the stroke is shown dotted. This is not usually necessary.)

15. The syllogism

(Premisses) { All financial bills are hotly debated
All financial bills are uncontroversial

(Conclusion) Some uncontroversial things are hotly debated

is shown as invalid by the following diagram.

financial bills

uncontroversial things

hotly-debated things

What additional existential premiss is needed to make it valid?

124

"There are financial bills".

16. Mark this diagram to represent the following syllogism, and say what additional existential premiss is needed to make it valid.

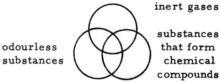

odourless substances

inert gases

substances that form chemical compounds

(Premisses) { No inert gases form chemical compounds
All inert gases are odourless

(Conclusion) { Some odourless substances do not form chemical compounds.

---

odourless substances

inert gases

substances that form chemical compounds

Extra premiss: "There are inert gases". (Stroke as marked.)

END OF CHAPTER 14

Chapter 15: Predicates and Quantifiers

The theory of syllogisms as dealt with in the previous two chapters, needs to be considerably extended to deal with more complex kinds of argument. This chapter indicates how this extension is effected in modern logic, by the logic of predicates and quantifiers.

1.   The logic of syllogisms is restricted to statements of four basic forms -- "All As are Bs", and so on -- each containing two terms. The previous chapter extended this to the extent of adding existential statements. However, it is clear that there are many other kinds of statement.

For one thing, we need to build a bridge between the logic of syllogisms and the logic of unanalysed statements considered in Part 2.

As a start, let us see what statements would look like if we were to analyse them into "subject" and "predicate". The easiest kind of statement to analyse in this way is one in which the "subject" is a proper name, representing a single person or thing; thus

"John is tall"
"Mary is fair"
"Julius Caesar was a great general"
    etc. etc.

The predicate in these cases is normally more-or-less the same thing as a class-term, of the kind that occurred in the theory of the syllogism. We shall use capital letters for predicates and small letters as proper names; for example

"T" for "tall" (or "is tall")
and "j" for "John".

We shall also put the predicate before the subject: thus, for

"John is tall" we write

Tj

and for "Mary is fair", with obvious meanings for

the letters, we write

$$Fm.$$

Writing "c" for "Julius Caesar" and "G" for "is a great general".
write "Julius Caesar is a great general".

Gc

2.   We can use this notation even when we do not have a "proper
name" in the strict sense of the word; for an individual person or
thing is often referred to by means of a longer descriptive phrase,
such as "The most illustrious of Britain's recent Prime Ministers"
or "The man who broke the bank at Monte Carlo". In the sentence
"The king of Spain's daughter came to visit me" what phrase represents
the "subject"; and what the "predicate"?

Subject: "The king of Spain's daughter"
Predicate: "came to visit me".

3.   A pair of letters such as "Tj" (for "John is tall") represents a
single statement. We can use truth-functional operators in connection
with these pairs exactly as we did earlier with single-letter statements
"S", "T" or "p", "q".
Thus

$$-Tj$$

means "John is not tall"
and if "m" stand for "Mary" and "F" for "fair"

$$Tj. Fm$$

means ....

"John is tall and Mary is fair".

4.   Similarly

$$Tj \ v \ Tm$$

means ....

"John is tall or Mary is tall" that is, "John or Mary is tall".

5. And
$$Tj. -Fj$$
means ....

"John is tall and John is not fair" or "John is tall but not fair".

6. We could, of course, mix the two notations. If "S" means "It is raining" and "C" means "has a coat", how would you write "It is raining and John has no coat"?

$S. -Cj$

7. In fact, from the purely logical point of view, the analysis of simple statements into subject and predicate does not achieve anything. The logical relation of "John is tall" to "John is fair" is indifference, and we might just as well symbolise them "S" and "T" respectively.

What is the relation of
$$\text{"John is tall"}$$
to "Mary is tall"?

Indifference.

8. Let "A" mean "is an Australian" and let "G" mean "is good-natured"; and let "s" mean "Smith".
Put into words:
$$As \supset Gs.$$

"If Smith is an Australian Smith is good-natured"

9. The previous example looks as if it has some connection with the generalisation "All Australians are good-natured". However, as it stands, it is simple a truth-function of "As" and "Gs", and can alternatively be written
$$-As \lor Gs$$

which means literally ....

"Either Smith is not an Australian or Smith is good-natured".

10.   The statement in the previous example in fact, would be simply
<u>true</u> if Smith were, say, an American. However, we are close to a
notation for "All As are Bs". What we need is a formulation such as
        "If <u>anyone</u> is an Australian, he is good-natured" or, better
        "If x is an Australian, x is good-natured (no matter who x may
be)",
Write "All nuclear submarines have long endurance"   in the form
just given.

"If x is a nuclear submarine x has long endurance (no matter what x may
be)."

11.   We shall use a notation of the form
                    $(x)(Ax \supset Bx)$
for statements such as "All As are Bs".
Here the part in the second bracket means "If x is an A, then x is a
B". The letter "x" is placed in brackets at the beginning to indicate
that it is a variable: we can read "(x)" as
                    "Whatever x may be .."
or, for short,
                    "For all x .."
Thus
            "For all x, if x is an A, x is a B".
Now how would you write "All Australians are good-natured" (using
"A" for "is an Australian", "G" for "is good-natured")?

$(x)(Ax \supset Gx)$

12.   "No Australians are good-natured" can be expressed "For all
x, if x is an Australian, x is <u>not</u> good-natured"; or
                $(x)(Ax \supset -Gx)$.
Write in symbols "No artificial satellites are atom-powered". (Use

"S" for "is an artificial satellite" and "P" for "is atom-powered")

(x)(Sx ⊃ -Px)

13. Write in symbols "No blast-furnaces are beauty-spots", using "F" for "is a blast-furnace" and "B" for "is a beauty-spot".

(x)(Fx ⊃ -Bx)

14. The symbol "(x)" is called a _quantifier_: in particular, it is a _universal quantifier_, because it is used to formulate "universal" statements; that is, statements involving all members of some class. ("All men are mortal" is a _universal_ statement because it is about all men.) It is easy to build universal statements of forms different from those given so far. For example, when the Greek philosopher Heraclitus said "Everything changes", he was uttering a universal statement which we could symbolise using "C" for "changes" as
$$(x)(Cx)$$
that is, "For all x, x changes". Express in symbols "Everything is either amusing or worthless", using "A" for "is amusing" and "W" for "is worthless".

(x)(Ax v Wx)

15. Or we can have a material implication whose antecedent or consequent is a truth-function.
"All successful politicians are hardworking" might need to be analysed using "S" for "is successful", "P" for "is a politician" and "H" for "is hardworking", so that it would come out as
$$(x)((Sx. Px) ⊃ Hx).$$
Write in symbols "Middle-aged men are bald but not bashful", using "M" for "is a middle-aged man", "B" for "is bald" and "S" for "is bashful".

(x)(Mx ⊃ (Bx. -Sx))

16. Write in symbols "Gamblers are either fools or rogues", using

"G", "F" and "R" for the appropriate predicates.

$(x)(Gx \supset (Fx \lor Rx))$

17. Besides the universal quantifier "(x)" (meaning "For all x") the existential quantifier, "(Ex)" is often used: this means "For at least one x". (The letter "E" is sometimes written backwards or upside-down to avoid confusing it with a predicate. We shall avoid using "E" as a predicate.)

     We normally use the existential quantifier with a simple conjunction. "At least one Australian is good-natured" becomes "For at least one x, x is Australian <u>and</u> x is good-natured", or
$$(Ex)(Ax. Gx)$$
Write in symbols "At least one mammal lives in the sea" using "M" for "is a mammal" and "S" for "lives in the sea".

$(Ex)(Mx. Sx)$

18. Write in symbols "At least one inert gas is radioactive", using "I" for "is inert", "G" for "is a gas" and "R" for "is radioactive".

$(Ex)(Ix. Gx. Rx)$

19. A simple existential statement such as "There are As" - strictly "There is at least one A" - will be written directly using an existential quantifier. Write "There is at least one mermaid", using "M" for "is a mermaid".

$(Ex)(Mx)$

20. We shall continue, for convenience, to use "Some" to mean "At least one". Which kind of quantifier - universal or existential - would we use to symbolise "Some businessmen are hardworking"?

Existential.

21. Which kind of quantifier would we use to symbolise "Every cloud has a silver lining?"

Universal.

22. Is there any relation between universal quantifiers and existential quantifiers?
The relation of "Some bears are marsupials"
to "No bears are marsupials"

is ....

---

contradiction.

23. "No bears are marsupials" can be written as the negation of "Some bears are marsupials". A whole quantified expression is a statement and we can negate it as we can any other statement. It follows that

$$(x)(Bx \supset -Mx)$$

is equivalent to

$$-(Ex)(Bx.Mx).$$

What is the contradictory of "All bears are marsupials"?

"Not all bears are marsupials" or "Some bears are not marsupials"

24. Write a formula to represent "It is not the case that some bears are not marsupials".

$-(Ex)(Bx. -Mx)$

25. Write in symbols "Not all Prime Ministers receive knighthoods", firstly, using an existential quantifier, and secondly, as "It is not the case that all Prime Ministers receive knighthoods". (Use "P" for "is a Prime Minister" and "K" for "receives a knighthood".)

$(Ex)(Px. -Kx)$
$-(x)(Px \supset Kx)$

26.   These equivalences can be derived from a simpler one which we can write schematically

"(x)" is equivalent to "-(Ex)-"

("For all x" is equivalent to "Not for some x not") and conversely

"(Ex)" is equivalent to "-(x)-".

Let us derive, from the first of these, the equivalence of $(x)(Ax \supset Bx)$ and $-(Ex)(Ax.-Bx)$. Directly, we can see that $(x)(Ax \supset Bx)$ is equivalent to $-(Ex)(-(Ax \supset Bx))$: can we show that $-(Ax \supset Bx)$ is equivalent to $Ax.-Bx$?

Show by means of a truth-table that $-(p \supset q)$ is equivalent to $p.-q$ (for any p and q).

p	q	p ⊃ q	-(p ⊃ q)	-q	p.-q
1	1				
1	0				
0	1				
0	0				

---

p	q	p ⊃ q	-(p ⊃ q)	-q	p.-q
1	1	1	0	0	0
1	0	0	1	1	1
0	1	1	0	0	0
0	0	1	0	1	0

The last and third last columns are identical.

27.   In fact, we originally defined "$p \supset q$" as $-(p.-q)$. Hence $Ax \supset Bx$ is equivalent to

$$-(Ax.-Bx)$$

so that $-(Ax \supset Bx)$ is equivalent to

$$-\left[-(Ax.-Bx)\right]$$

which is equivalent by the law of double negation, to $Ax.-Bx$.

Hence $(x)(Ax \supset Bx)$ is equivalent to $-(Ex)(Ax.-Bx)$.

We can write this equivalence directly as a formula: we have, in effect, proved that

$$(x)(Ax \supset Bx) \equiv -(Ex)(Ax.-Bx)$$

is a tautology.

Write a similar formula for $(x)(Ax \supset -Bx)$.

$(x)(Ax \supset -Bx) \equiv$ ....

$(x)(Ax \supset -Bx) \equiv -(Ex)(Ax. Bx)$

28. It is not the function of this course to give a complete account of the logic of predicates. However, let us see how syllogisms may be dealt with, and how this kind of reasoning may be generalised.

Taking the example

(Premisses) { All men are mortal
All Greeks are men
(Conclusion) All Greeks are mortal

with "M" for "is a man", "O" for "is mortal" and "G" for "is a Greek", we see that in symbols it is

(Premisses) { $(x)(Mx \supset Ox)$
$(x)(Gx \supset Mx)$
(Conclusion) $(x)(Gx \supset Ox)$

We want to develop a rule in accordance with which the conjunction of the premisses implies the conclusion; that is

$$[(x)(Mx \supset Ox).(x)(Gx \supset Mx)] \supset (x)(Gx \supset Ox).$$

Write a similar formula for the syllogism

(Premisses) { No one who reads Plato dislikes him
All philosophy students read Plato
(Conclusion) No philosophy students dislike Plato.

(Use "R" for "reads Plato", "D" for "dislikes Plato", "S" for "is a philosophy student".)

$$[(x)(Rx \supset -Dx).(x)(Sx \supset Rx)] \supset (x)(Sx \supset -Dx)$$
(Be careful about bracketing.)

29. We shall introduce two rules which are sufficient for dealing with this syllogism. The first is that when we have a conjunction of two expressions which both have <u>universal</u> quantifiers, the two may be put together under a single quantifier. If "$(x)(f_1)$" and "$(x)(f_2)$" are two formulae, where f_1 and f_2 are arbitrary expressions containing x, we write

$$[(x)(f_1).(x)(f_2)] \equiv (x)(f_1 \cdot f_2)$$

As an application of this rule the conjunction of the two premisses of our syllogism can be simplified: the formula

$$(x)(Mx \supset Ox).(x)(Gx \supset Mx)$$

is equivalent to $(x)[(Mx \supset Ox).(Gx \supset Mx)]$

Do the same for the other syllogism in the previous example: that is,

simplify the conjunction
$$(x)(Rx \supset -Dx).(x)(Sx \supset Rx).$$

$(x)[(Rx \supset -Dx).(Sx \supset Rx)]$
(Again, be careful about bracketing.)

30.   The second rule is that we can conduct inference-processes in a quantified expression exactly as if the quantifier were not there. If a formula f_1 implies another formula f_2, then the quantified formula $(x)(f_1)$ implies the quantified formula $(x)(f_2)$. The same rule holds for existential quantifiers: $(Ex)(f_1)$ implies $(Ex)(f_2)$.

Now, by the "chain rule" for material implication;
$$(Mx \supset Ox).(Gx \supset Mx) \quad \underline{implies} \ Gx \supset Ox.$$
Consequently
$$(x)[(Mx \supset Ox).(Gx \supset Mx)] \quad \underline{implies} \ (x)(Gx \supset Ox).$$
Use the same rule to draw a conclusion from
$$(x)[(Rx \supset -Dx).(Sx \supset Rx)].$$
(Set it out as we have set out the first example.)

$(Rx \supset -Dx).(Sx \supset Rx) \quad \underline{implies} \ Sx \supset -Dx$
Consequently
$(x)[(Rx \supset -Dx).(Sx \supset Rx)] \quad \underline{implies} \ (x)(Sx \supset Dx).$

31.   The two rules are enough to validate the syllogisms in the examples given. Thus to show that "All men are mortal and all Greeks are men" implies "All Greeks are mortal" we proceed as follows:
$$(x)(Mx \supset Ox).(x)(Gx \supset Mx)$$
is equivalent by rule 1 to
$$(x)[(Mx \supset Ox).(Gx \supset Mx)]$$
which implies, by rule 2
$$(x)(Gx \supset Ox).$$
The syllogism

(Premisses) $\begin{cases} \text{All criminals are psychopaths} \\ \text{No scientists are criminals} \end{cases}$

(Conclusion) No scientists are psychopaths

is <u>invalid</u>. Set it out in the same way (using "C", "P" and "S") and say why it is <u>not</u> validated by the rules.

135

(x)(Cx ⊃ Px).(x)(Sx ⊃ -Cx) is equivalent by rule 1 to
(x)[(Cx ⊃ Px).(Sx ⊃ -Cx)]
but this does <u>not</u> imply (x)(Sx ⊃ -Px) because
(Cx ⊃ Px).(Sx ⊃ -Cx) does not imply Sx ⊃ -Px.

32. Now let us add a rule to deal with mixed universal and existential quantifiers.
First, taking the example

(Premisses) { All mammals are warm-blooded
{ Some sea creatures are mammals
(Conclusion) Some sea creatures are warm-blooded

-- write a formula expressing the fact that the premisses imply the the conclusion. (Use "M", "W" and "S" for the predicates.)

[(x)(Mx ⊃ Wx).(Ex)(Sx.Mx)] ⊃ (Ex)(Sx.Wx)

33. Let f_1 and f_2 be, as before, two expressions containing x. If f_1 is true for <u>all</u> x and f_2 is true for <u>some</u> x, f_1 must be true for those x's for which f_2 is true; and hence, for some x, f_1 and f_2 are both true.

In symbols: the conjunction
$$(x)(f_1).(Ex)(f_2)$$
implies
$$(Ex)(f_1.f_2)$$
As an application of this we can say that the conjunction of premisses
$$(x)(Mx ⊃ Wx).(Ex)(Sx.Mx)$$
implies
$$(Ex)[(Mx ⊃ Wx).Sx.Mx]$$
Write a similar implication for the pair of premisses

{ All doctors are graduates
{ Some hospital employees are not graduates.
using the letters "D", "G" and "H".

(x)(Dx ⊃ Gx).(Ex)(Hx.-Gx) implies (Ex)(Dx ⊃ Gx).Hx.-Gx

34. We have already specified by rule 2 that an inference may be

carried out under a quantifier. In the expression
$$(Ex)[(Mx \supset Wx).Sx.Mx]$$
it may be noticed that we have premisses $Mx \supset Wx$ and Mx from which, by the rule of modus ponens, we can deduce Wx. Consequently the expression as a whole implies
$$(Ex)(Sx.Wx)$$
In the case of the second syllogism in the previous example, show how to validate the conclusion

Some hospital employees are not doctors.

From $Dx \supset Gx$ (which is equivalent to $-Gx \supset -Dx$) and $-Gx$ we deduce $-Dx$.
Consequently from $(Ex)[(Dx \supset Gx).Hx.-Gx]$ we deduce $(Ex)(Hx.-Dx)$.

35. Show that the rules do <u>not</u> validate the invalid syllogism

(Premisses) { All lawyers are graduates
{ Some graduates are dishonest
(Conclusion) Some lawyers are dishonest.

(Use "L", "G" and "D".)

$(x)(Lx \supset Gx).(Ex)(Gx.Dx)$
implies
$(Ex)[(Lx \supset Gx).Gx.Dx]$
but $Lx \supset Gx$ and Gx do <u>not</u> imply Lx and so the rules do not validate $(Ex)(Lx.Dx)$.

36. The inference

(Premisses) { All astrologers are either fools or charlatans
{ Not all astrologers are fools.
(Conclusion) Some charlatans are not fools

is not a syllogism in the strict sense, since the first premiss contains all three terms, in the form (with obvious meanings)
$$(x)[Ax \supset (Fx \lor Cx)]$$
Show, however, that it can be validated by the rules.

(x)(Ax ⊃ (Fx v Cx)).(Ex)(Ax. -Fx)
implies
(Ex){[Ax ⊃ (Fx v Cx)]. Ax. -Fx}.
Now Ax ⊃ (Fx v Cx) and Ax together imply Fx v Cx and with -Fx this implies Cx. -Fx. Consequently the premisses imply the conclusion (Ex)(Cx. -Fx).

END OF CHAPTER 15

(Those who have worked through chapter 14 may wish to try out the rules on some of the examples given in it.)

Chapter 16: The Elementary Logic of Relations

This chapter introduces "two-place" predicates and multiple quantification.
The definitions of reflexivity, symmetry and transitivity of relations are given and logical relations are used as examples.

1. We have been using capital letters to represent what we called predicates; and we conceived predicates to resemble the "terms" met with in the theory of the syllogism. Thus, using "M" for "is a man" and "O" for "is mortal", we symbolised
"All men are mortal"
in the form . . . .

$(x)(Mx \supset Ox)$

2. The word "predicate" is also a grammatical term: statements are analysed, in grammar as in logic, into subject and predicate. Thus writing "T" for "is tall" and "j" for "John" we symbolise "John is tall" as . . . .

Tj

3. Now let us alter our conception of "predicates" a little. Sometimes a sentence can be turned completely round without changing its meaning in any essential way. Thus the sentence
"Amanda wore a dress with red sequins on it"

can be turned round and put in the form

"There were red sequins on the dress Amanda wore".

In the first form, it can be easily analysed into subject and predicate, the subject being "Amanda".

There is, however, no reason to refuse to analyse the second form in the same way: the subject is "Amanda" and the predicate is

"There were red sequins on the dress ...... wore".

where the row of dashes indicates the point at which the subject is to be inserted.

Under this new conception, a predicate is a <u>statement with a name-gap in it</u>.

Turn round the predicate "........ owns the slowest car of any student on the campus" so that it reads "No car ....".

(Say)

"No car of any other student on the campus is as slow as that owned by ...."

4. Instead of such devices as a row of dashes it is convenient to use a variable such as "x": thus we can speak of the predicate

"x gained top marks"

or

"Top marks were gained by x".

This way of writing things is virtually indispensible when we come to consider "two-place predicates"; that is, statements with <u>two</u> gaps in them. Consider the predicate

"x is the father of y".

which we might symbolise "Fxy". Write in symbols

"Andrew is the father of Brenda"

using "a" for "Andrew" and "b" for "Brenda".

Fab

5. We shall also speak of a two-place predicate as a <u>relation</u>. In the example "Andrew is the father of Brenda" it is obvious that a "relation" between the individuals Andrew and Brenda is specified. It should be remembered, however, that there is nothing formally wrong with applying the same symbolism in cases such as

"Andrew is a plumber and Brenda is a typist"

where no "relation", in the ordinary sense, is indicated. Writing

"Px" for "x is a plumber" and "Tx" for "x is a typist", how would you symbolise
"Andrew, who is a plumber, is the father of Brenda, who is a typist"?

Pa. Fab. Tb
(The order of the conjuncts is immaterial.)

6. Writing "Wxy" for "x works for the same firm as y's husband", express in symbols
"Andrew is Brenda's father and works for the same firm as her husband"

Fab. Wab

7. The statement
"Brenda works for the same firm as her husband"
can be expressed, a little clumsily, as
"Brenda works for the same firm as Brenda's husband".
If "Wxy" means, as before, "x works for the same firm as y's husband", and "b" stands for "Brenda", express this in symbols.

Wbb

8. Now let us bring quantifiers into the picture. When we have two variables we can quantify with respect to one variable or both. If we quantify with respect to one variable only, we get, in effect, a one-place predicate left.
For example, let "Fxy" mean "x is the father of y".
The expression

$$(Ey)(Fxy)$$

means
"There is a y such that x is the father of y"
or
"x is someone's father".
Writing "a" for "Andrew", how would you write
"Andrew is someone's father"?

(Ey)(Fay)
(<u>or</u> (Ex)(Fax))

    9.   Notice that when we have only one variable, and it stands under a quantifier, <u>it does not matter whether it is x or y</u>: all that matters is that, when more than one variable occurs, a distinction is made between them.
What does

$$(Ex)(Fxb)$$

mean (where "b" stands for "Brenda")?

"Brenda has a father"

    10.   Still using "Wxy" to mean "x works for the same firm as y's husband", what does

$$(Ex)(Fxb. Wxb)$$

mean?

"Brenda has a father who works for the same firm as her husband"

    11.   "(Ey)(Fay)" means "Andrew has a father"
and   "(Ey)(Fby)" means "Brenda has a father".
What does

$$(x)(Ey)(Fxy)$$

mean?

"Everyone has a father"

    12.   Let "Rxy" mean "x has read y": we shall assume that the "x" is the name of a person and the "y" the name of a book. Writing "s" for "Smith" and "w" for "<u>War and Peace</u>", symbolise
          (1) "Smith has read <u>War and Peace</u>".
          (2) "Smith has read something".
          (3) "Someone has read something".

---

(1)   Rsw
(2)   (Ey)(Rsy)   (or (Ex)(Rsx), etc.)
(3)   (Ex)(Ey)(Rxy) (or (Ey)(Ex)(Ryx), etc.)

    13.   With the same meanings for the letters, symbolise
              (1) "Smith has read everything".
              (2) "Someone has read everything".

---

(1) (y)(Rsy)   (or (Ex)(Rsx), etc.)
(2) (Ex)(y)(Rxy) (or (Ey)(Ex)(Ryx), etc.)

    14.   (x)(y)(Rxy) means "For all x, for all y, x has ready, or
                 "Everyone has read everything"
Suppose we change the order of the quantifiers, getting
                 (y)(x)(Rxy)
which means "For all y, for all x, x has read y", or
           "Everything has been read by everyone".
Do these differ in meaning?

No.

    15.   (Ex)(Ey)(Rxy) means "Someone has read something".
          (Ey)(Ex)(Rxy) means "Something has been read by someone".
Do these differ in meaning, or are they equivalent?

They are equivalent.

    16.   In ordinary speech, however, we are not always as careful as
we should be to distinguish between, say
              "Everyone has read something"
and
         "There is something that everyone has read".
In the second case it is implied that there is some particular thing
that has been read by everybody, whereas the first of the two statements would be true if there were no such thing, so long as different
people had each read something or other.
    Symbolise each of the statements.

(x)(Ey)(Rxy)
(Ey)(x)(Rxy)
(<u>in that order</u>)

17.   The statement "You can fool all of the people some of the time" can mean either
              (1) "Everyone can be fooled occasionally"
or   (2) "You can sometimes fool everyone at once".
Writing "Fxt" for "You can fool x at time t", express each of these in symbols.

(x)(Et)(Fxt)
(Et)(x)(Fxt)
(<u>in that order</u>. <u>Nomenclature for "x" and "t" is, of course, immaterial.</u>)

18.   If "Cxy" means "x is a cause of y", put clearly into words:
              (1) (y)(Ex)(Cxy)
              (2) (Ex)(y)(Cxy)

(Say:)
(1) "Everything has some cause or other"
(2) "There is something which is the cause of everything"

19.   There is a relation of implication between pairs of statements as in the last example.
Does (1) imply (2), or does (2) imply (1)?

---

(2) implies (1)

20.   If x is a parent of y and y is a parent of z, x is a grandparent of z: generally, x is a grandparent of z if x is a parent of <u>someone</u> who is a parent of z, or (with "Pxy" for "x is a parent of y")
              (Ey)(Pxy. Pyz)
Writing "Fxy" for "x is a friend of y", how would you write
              "x is a friend of a friend of z"?

(Ey)(Fxy. Fyz)

    21.   How would you write
                "x and y have a parent in common"?
    ("Pxy" for "x is a parent of y")

(Ez)(Pzx. Pzy)

    22.   Further extensions of this kind of formulation are, of course, possible. Thus "x is a great-grandparent of y" becomes, say,
                (Ez)(Ew)(Pxz. Pzw. Pwy)
How would you write
             "Andrew is someone's grandparent"?
("a" for "Andrew".)

(Ex)(Ey)(Pax. Pxy)

    23.   How would you write
             "Everyone has a grandparent"?

(x)(Ey)(Ez)(Pyz. Pzx)

    24.   If "Gxyz" means "x gave y to z", and "s" and "j" are "Smith" and "Jones" respectively, express in symbols
             "Smith gave something to Jones."

(Ey)(Gsyj)

    25. With the same meanings, express in symbols
             "Smith gave something to everyone"
on the assumption that Smith gave a number of individual presents rather than one collective one.

(z)(Ey)(Gsyz)

26.   A relation Rxy is called symmetrical if, whenever x has this relation to y, y also has it to x.

"Classmate of" is a symmetrical relation, because whenever x is a classmate of y, y is also a classmate of x.

"Brother of" is not symmetrical, since if x is a brother of y, y may be a sister, not brother, of x.   We have met this distinction before in connection with logical relations.

The relation of contrariety is ....
The relation of implication is ....

---

symmetrical.
not symmetrical.
(<u>in that order</u>)

27.   The condition that the relation Ṙxy be symmetrical can be put in symbols in the following formulation: "For all x and y, if x has the relation R to y then y has the relation R to x".   Symbolise ·this, using material implication for "if....then".

(x)(y)(Rxy ⊃ Ryx)

28.   A relation is called antisymmetrical if, when x has it to y, y definitely does not have it to x.
Put this condition in symbols.

(x)(y)(Rxy ⊃ -Ryx)

29.   A relation is called <u>reflexive</u> if everything has it to itself.
"Child of the same parent as" is reflexive.

Put the defining condition in symbols.

(x)(Rxx)

30.   Which logical relation is reflexive?

146

Equivalence.

31. We have also met <u>transitive</u> relations: a relation is transitive if, when x has it to y and y has it to z, x has it to z.
Put this condition in symbols.

$(x)(y)(z)[(Rxy.Ryz) \supset Rxz]$

32. Which three of the logical relations are transitive?

Superimplication
Subimplication
Equivalence.   OMIT to end of chapter

33. Material implication can be considered as a ."relation" in the rather extended sense in which the word is used in this chapter.
It is clearly transitive by the chain rule:
$$[(p \supset q)(p \supset r)] \supset (p \supset r).$$
This would be exactly in accordance with our definition of transitivity if we were to put quantifiers in: thus
$$(p)(q)(r)\{[(p \supset q).(q \supset r)] \supset (p \supset r)\}$$
In fact, when we assert that a given truth-functional statement is a tautology we are, in effect, saying that it is true for all statements; that is, whatever is put for the variables $p, q, \ldots$
Write, using quantifiers, a formula specifying that conjunction is symmetrical.

$(p)(q)[(p.q) \supset (q.p)]$

34. We can express that a given formula is <u>not</u> a tautology by saying that for some $p, q, \ldots$ it is false. For example, we can express
"p.q is not a tautology"
in the form $(Ep)(Eq)[-(p.q)]$.
Write in symbols "p is not a tautology".

$(Ep)(-p)$

147

35.   In particular, we can write "p does not imply q" in the form
         "For some p and q, p is true and q is false".
Express in symbols the fact that material implication is not
symmetrical; that is, that p ⊃ q does not imply q ⊃ p.

$(Ep)(Eq)[(p \supset q) . -(q \supset p)]$

36.   Is material implication reflexive?   Formulate in symbols the
assertion that material implication is not reflexive, and say whether
it is true or false.

$(Ep)[-(p \supset p)]$
False: material implication is reflexive.

END OF CHAPTER 16

END OF PART 3

148

Revision Chapter 1: Logical Relations

This chapter is designed for the revision of the material of chapters 1 - 4 of the main part of the course.

    1.   Two statements S and T are called <u>contradictories</u> if they are so related that they cannot both be true and cannot both be false. If they <u>can</u> both be false they are called . . . .

---

contraries.

    2.   The statements
"Smith is present"
and "Smith is not present

are . . . .

---

contradictories.

    3.   The statements
"Smith is in Melbourne"
and "Smith is in Sydney"

are . . . .

---

contraries.

    4.   Contradictories are said to stand to one another in the relation of . . . .

contradiction.

5.   Contraries are said to stand to one another in the relation of
. . . .

contrariety.

6.   Contradictories and contraries are both related such that if one statement is .... the other is .....

true, false
(<u>in that order</u>)

7.   Contradiction and contrariety are two kinds of logical relation between statements. How many such kinds are there altogether?

Seven.

8.   Two statements are said to be <u>indifferent</u> when nothing about the truth or falsity of the one follows from the truth or falsity of the other; and the relation between them is then said to be . . . .

indifference.

9.   Two statements are said to be <u>equivalent</u> when the truth of one implies the truth of the other and <u>vice versa</u>; and the relation between them is called . . . .

equivalence.

10.   The relation of
         "There are three chairs in the room"
       to "There are four tables in the room"
is . . . .

indifference.

11. The relation of
"There is at least one unscaled Tibetan
mountain-peak"
to "Not all mountain-peaks in Tibet have
been scaled"
is . . . .

---

equivalence.

12. If, in a statement of the form "No As are Bs", the terms "A"
and "B" are transposed, the logical relation to the original statement
is . . . .

---

equivalence.

13. If, in a statement of the form "All As are Bs", the terms "A"
and "B" are transposed, the logical relation to the original statement
is . . . .

---

indifference.

14. Logical relations, as we here understand them, do not hold
between _terms_ but only between . . . .

---

statements.

15. What is the relation of
"At least some bears are marsupials"
to "At least some marsupials are bears"?

Equivalence.

16. Can the logical relation of S to T be discovered without knowing

the actual truth or falsity of S or T ?

Yes.

17.   When two statements S and T are contraries there is at least
one other statement U that is contrary to both of them.
A statement contrary to both
                    "X is greater than Y"
              and "X is less then Y"
is "X is ...."

---

equal to Y

18.   A statement contrary to both
              "It is raining in both Sydney and Melbourne"
        and "It is raining in Sydney but not in Melbourne"
is "It .... in Sydney"

---

is not raining

19.   What are the <u>possible alternative</u> relations of S to T when S and
T cannot both be true?

Contradiction
Contrariety
(<u>in either order</u>)

20.   The way the distinguish contradiction from contrariety is to
ask "Can both statements be (true, false)?" (Which?)

---

false

21.   If two statements cannot both be false but can both be true they
are called <u>subcontraries</u>, and the relation between them is
....

---

subcontrariety.

22. What are the <u>possible alternative</u> relations of S to T when S and T cannot both be false?

Contradiction
Subcontrariety
(<u>in either order</u>)

23. If empty terms are not permitted, what is the relation of
"At least one planet is inhabited"
to "At least one planet is uninhabited"?

Subcontrariety.

24. The following is a part of a "square of opposition":

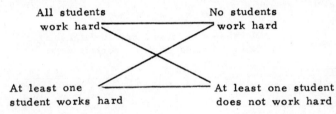

All students
work hard

No students
work hard

At least one
student works hard

At least one student
does not work hard

Assuming there are no complications concerning empty terms, what is the relation on the upper side? on the lower side? on the diagonals?

Contrariety
Subcontrariety
Contradiction
(<u>in that order</u>)

25. Let us complete the square of opposition. We say that "All students work hard" <u>implies</u> "At least one student works hard", and the relation is called <u>implication</u>. However, if S implies T, T does not necessarily imply S; that is to say, the relation of implication is not . . . .

---

symmetrical.

26. If S implies T we say that the relation of S to T is superimplication and the relation of T to S is subimplication. The relation
of

"All students work hard"
to "At least one student works hard"
is ....

---

superimplication.

27. What is the relation of
"At least one planet is inhabited"
to "All planets are inhabited"?

Subimplication.

28. What is the relation of
"No whales swim in tropical waters"
to "Not all whales swim in tropical waters"?

Superimplication.

29. Draw a "square of opposition" with "All fish have ears" at the
top left-hand corner, and indicate all the logical relations.
Indicate implication by an arrow on the appropriate line.

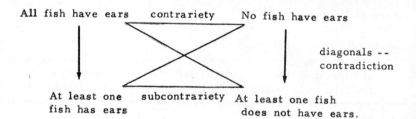

All fish have ears   contrariety   No fish have ears

diagonals --
contradiction

At least one   subcontrariety   At least one fish
fish has ears   does not have ears.

30. What is the relation of
"All As are Bs"
to "All Bs are As"?

Indifference.

31. What is the relation of a statement to its negation?

Contradiction.

32. A good general method of forming the negation of a statement is to prefix it by "It is not the case that". This is because this phrase usually converts it into a statement which is .... when the original statement is ....., and _vice versa_.

---

true, false
(in either order)

33. What is the relation of
"Both of the Romans who courted Cleopatra
were killed in battle"
to "Neither of the Romans who courted Cleopatra
was killed in battle"?

Contrariety.

34. To determine the relation between a pair of statements we may start by asking ourselves "Is it some kind of implication?", taking this to include equivalence.
If the answer to this question is "No", what are the possible relations?

Contradiction
Contrariety
Subcontrariety
(in any order)

35.   Alternatively, we might start by asking "Can they both be true?" and "Can they both be false?". What are the possible relations corresponding with a "Yes" answer to <u>both</u> questions?

Superimplication
Subimplication
Equivalence
Indifference
(<u>in any order</u>)

36.   What is the relation of
        "Carbon has a lower conductivity than any metal"
    to "There is at least one metal with conductivity no
        higher than that of carbon"?

Contradiction .

37.   What is the relation of
"It is impossible to gain access to coal under Sydney Harbour" to
"There is no coal under Sydney Harbour"?

Subimplication.

38.   What is the relation of
        "In modern times a large house is a status symbol"
    to "Large houses have not always been status symbols
        in the past"?

Indifference.

39.   What is the relation of
            "At least twenty attended the lecture"
        to "Not more than twenty-five attended the lecture"?

Subcontrariety.

40. What is the relation of
    "Few positivists believe in free will"
    to "Most of those who do not believe in free
    will are positivists"?

Indifference.

41. What is the relation of
    "Mistakes in speech and writing are due
    to repressed thoughts"
    to "It is not only uneducted people that make
    mistakes in speech and writing"?

Indifference.

42. Does knowledge of the logical relation between two statements
ever give us any knowledge of the truth or falsity of the statements
themselves?

No.

END OF REVISION CHAPTER 1

Revision Chapter 2: The Logic of Unanalysed Statements

This chapter is designed for revision of the material of chapters 6-10 of the main part of the course.

1.   Statements may be either <u>simple</u> or <u>compound</u>.
A compound statement is one which is made up of simple statements. Since the statement "Either Wellington was a great general or Napoleon was unlucky" is made up of the statements "Wellington was a great general" and "Napoleon was unlucky" it is (simple, compound). (Which?)

---

compound.

2.   Amongst compound statements we are particularly interested in <u>truth-functional</u> compounds.   These are statements whose truth or falsity can be determined from the truth or falsity of their components. The statement
    "Napoleon was unlucky and lost the battle of Waterloo"
is a compound of the two statements . . . .

"Napoleon was unlucky" and
"Napoleon lost the battle of Waterloo".

3.   This compound is a <u>truth-functional</u> one because if we know, say, that the statement "Napoleon was unlucky" is true and the statement "Napoleon lost the battle of Waterloo" is true, we know that the

statement "Napoleon was unlucky and lost the battle of Waterloo" is
. . . .

---

true.

4.   The statement "Napoleon lost Waterloo <u>because</u> he was unlucky"
is a compound (in some sense) of the statements "Napoleon lost
Waterloo" and "Napoleon was unlucky"; but it is not a truth-functioanl
compound, because, although we know (say) that the two component
statements are true, we do not know from this alone . . . .
(Complete the sentence.)

(In suitable words)
whether the statement "Napoleon lost Waterloo <u>because</u> he was unlucky"
is true or false.

5.   <u>Negation</u>, <u>conjunction</u> and <u>disjunction</u> are t r u t h - f u n c t i o n a l
concepts.
The negation "-S" of a statement S is a statement which is
        true when S is false, and
        . . . . . when S is . . . .

---

false,
true
(<u>in that order</u>)

6.   Which of the following are negations of the statement "All wharf-
labourers are Communists"?
        (1) "Quite a lot of wharf-labourers are non-Communists"?
        (2) "Wharf-labourers are not all Communists"?
        (3) "There is at least one non-Communist wharf-labourer"?
        (4) "Some wharf-labourers are Communists"?
        (5) "It is not true that every wharf-labourer is a Communist"?
(Write the number or numbers.)

---

(2),   (3),   (5)

159

7.   "--S" is the negation of the negation of S.
The logical relation of --S to S is ....

---

equivalence.

8.   Truth-functions can be defined by <u>truth-tables</u>. Using "1" for "true" and "0" for "false", complete the following defining table for negation.

When S is	-S is
1	
0	

When S is	-S is
1	0
0	1

9.   The <u>conjunction</u> "S.T" ("S and T") of two statements S and T is a statement which is true when, and only when, S and T are both true.
Complete the following defining table for conjunction. (We head the columns just "S", "T" etc.)

S	T	S.T
1	1	
1	0	
0	1	
0	0	

S	T	S.T
1	1	1
1	0	0
0	1	0
0	0	0

160

10.   The word "and" usually, but not always, indicates a conjunction.
In which of the following cases is there a (simple) conjunction of two
statements?

     (1)   There are two lecturers and eight
          students at the meeting.

     (2)   There are 10 lecturers and students
          at the meeting.

     (3)   Smith and his wife work for the same
          firm.

     (4)   Smith and his wife have their birthdays
          in May.

     (5)   Smith, but not Jones, is a member of the
          Regiment.

(Write the number or numbers.)

---

(1), (4), (5)

11.   Complete the following truth-table in which the values of "S.-T"
("S and not T") are calculated.

S	T	-T	S.-T
1	1		
1	0		
0	1		
0	0		

S	T	-T	S.-T
1	1	0	0
1	0	1	1
0	1	0	0
0	0	1	0

12.   A triple conjunction of S, T and U can be written
$$S.T.U$$
being short for, say, (S.T).U.
If S means "There was petrol", T means "There was a spark" and U
means "The engine fired", write a formula to represent
        "There was petrol and there was a spark
          but the engine did not fire".

---

13.   If the arrow symbol " → " represents implication, which of the following are valid?

(1)   S. T → S ?
(2)   S. T → T ?
(3)   S. -T → S ?
(4)   S. -T → T ?

(Write the number or numbers.)

---

(1),   (2),   (3)

14.   In which of the following cases is -(S. T) true?

(1)   When S and T are both false ?
(2)   When S is false and T true ?
(3)   When S is true and T false ?
(4)   When S and T are both true ?

(Write the number or numbers.)

---

(1),   (2),   (3)

15.   The disjunction "S v T" ("S or T") of two statements S and T is a statement which is true when, and only when, either S or T is true. We shall understand this in the "non-exclusive" sense, such that S v T counts as true also if S and T are both true.

Complete the following truth-table for (non-exclusive) disjunction.

S	T	S v T
1	1	
1	0	
0	1	
0	0	

S	T	S v T
1	1	1
1	0	1
0	1	1
0	0	0

16. The formula

$$S \vee (T . U)$$

means

"Either S is true, or T and U are true".

Whereas the formula

$$(S \vee T) . U$$

means "..............................."

(In suitable words:)
"Either S or T is true, and U is true".

17. In which of the following cases is $-(S \vee T)$ true?
          (1) When S and T are both false ?
          (2) When S is false and T true ?
          (3) When S is true and T false ?
          (4) When S and T are both true ?

(Write the number or numbers.)

---

(1).

18. Using " $\rightarrow$ " for implication, write in symbols
"The conjunction of S and T implies the disjunction of S and T".
Is this true?

$S . T \rightarrow S \vee T$
Yes: true.

19. Using the two - way arrow " $\leftrightarrow$ " for equivalence, write in symbols
"The conjunction of S and T is equivalent to the negation of the disjunction of -S and -T".
Is this true?

$S . T \leftrightarrow -(-S \vee -T)$
Yes: true.

20. If S is true and T and U are false, which of the following are true?

> (1) -S v T v -U ?
> (2) (-S v -T). -U ?
> (3) (-S v -T). U ?

(Write the number or numbers, or "None".)

---

(1), (2)

21. If S is true, S v T is true independently of whether T is. Consequently the implication

$$S \rightarrow S \text{ v } T$$

is valid.

> Which of the following implications are valid?
> (1) S → S v -T ?
> (2) S.-T → S v -T ?
> (3) S.-T → (S.-T) v U ?

(Write the number or numbers, or "None".)

---

(1), (2), (3)

22. An arrow with a stroke through it, "↛", means "does not imply". If p represents the statement "S.T" and q represents "S", which of the following are true?

> (1) p → q ?
> (2) p ↛ q ?
> (3) q → p ?
> (4) q ↛ p ?

(Write the number or numbers.)

---

(1), (4)

23. In which of the following cases, if any, is "p → q" true?

> (1) p represents "-S v -T", q represents
>   "-S.-T" ?
> (2) p and q both represent "S v T v U" ?
> (3) p represents "Travel is expensive but rewarding"

164

and q represents "Travel is expensive but not rewarding" ?

---

(2)

24. The implication

$$-q \longrightarrow -p$$

is equivalent to the implication $p \longrightarrow q$, and this is called the <u>contraposed</u> (or <u>contrapositive</u>) form of the inference.
To contrapose an implication you interchange the two sides and negate both of them.

Write a formula representing the c o n t r a p o s e d form of the implication

$$S \longrightarrow S \vee T.$$

$-(S \vee T) \longrightarrow -S$

25. "$p \longrightarrow q$" is true if, whenever p is . . . . , it is not possible for q, at the same time, to be . . . . .

---

true
false
(<u>in that order</u>)

26. What features of the following truth-table for S.T and S v T indicate that S.T implies S v T?

S	T	S.T	S v T
1	1	1	1
1	0	0	1
0	1	0	1
0	0	0	0

(In suitable words:)
In row no. 1, which is the only row in which S.T is true, S v T is true also.

27.   Let us suppose that we know that p and q are truth-functions of S and T but that all that we know about them is their truth-table, which is as follows"

S	T	p	q
1	1	1	1
1	0	0	1
0	1	0	0
0	0	1	1

Does either imply the other?
Does either imply S or T?

---

p implies q.
Neither implies S or T.

28.   If p <u>does not</u> imply q, this will be shown in their truth-table by the fact that in at least one row p is .... and q is .....

---

true
false
(<u>in that order</u>)

29.   The material implication "S ⊃ T" (say just "S implies T" or "If S then T", so long as no confusion arises) is a truth-function of S and T such that it is

          false when S is true and T false,
          and true otherwise.

Complete the following defining table:

S	T	S ⊃ T
1	1	
1	0	
0	1	
0	0	

S	T	S ⊃ T
1	1	1
1	0	0
0	1	1
0	0	1

30.　If p implies q there is no row of their truth-table with p true and q false.　It follows that if a table for the material implication p ⊃ q is calculated it will . . . .

It will have all 1 s.

31.　Let us suppose that p and q are truth-functions of S, T and U so that p ⊃ q is also, indirectly, a truth-function of S, T and U. A table for p and q is given below.　Add a column for p ⊃ q.

p	q	p ⊃ q
1	1	
1	0	
1	0	
0	1	
0	1	
1	0	
0	0	
0	0	

The column for p ⊃ q should read "1 - 0 - 0 - 1 - 1 - 0 - 1 - 1".

32.　In the previous example, which rows indicate that p does not imply q, and why?

Rows 2, 3 and 6, because p ⊃ q has the value 0 in these rows.

33.　Two statements are equivalent if each implies the other.　If p and q are equivalent, p must be true whenever q is, and q must be true whenever p is.　In other words, they must have the same value under all circumstances.

　　Complete the following truth-table and say what equivalences you find.

S	T	S v T	S.(S v T)	S.T	T v (S.T)

S. (S v T) is equivalent to S.

T v (S. T) is equivalent to T.

34. The material equivalence "S ≡ T" of S and T is a truth-function which is true when S and T have the same value, false otherwise. Complete the following defining table.

S	T	S ≡ T
1	1	
1	0	
0	1	
0	0	

S	T	S ≡ T
1	1	1
1	0	0
0	1	0
0	0	1

35. Complete the following truth-table for p ≡ q, where p and q are supposed to be truth-functions of, say, S, T and U.

p	q	p ≡ q
1	1	
1	0	
1	1	
0	0	
0	0	
1	1	
1	1	
0	1	

The column should read "1 - 0 - 1 - 1 - 1 - 1 - 1 - 0".

36. Complete the following table for (S. T) v (-S. -T). To what simpler formula is it equivalent?

S	T	S. T	-S	-T	-S. -T	(S. T) v (-S. -T)
1	1					
1	0					
0	1					
0	0					

168

The final column should read "1 - 0 - 0 - 1".
The formula is equivalent to $S \equiv T$.

37.   The equivalence just noted could be indicated by the fact that a certain formula has all 1's in its table.   What formula?

$(S \equiv T) \equiv [(S . T) v (-S. -T)]$
or $[(S. T) v (-S. -T)] \equiv (S \equiv T)$
(Note bracketing.)

38.   A formula that has all 1's in its table is called a <u>tautology</u>, and a formula that has all 0's is called a <u>self-contradiction</u>. Which of the following are tautologies?

(1) $S v -S$?
(2) $(S . T) v (-S. -T)$?
(3) $(S. T) \supset S$?
(4) $(S. (S \supset T)) \supset T$?
(5) $S \supset (S v T)$?

(Write the number or numbers, or "None")

---

(1), (3), (4), (5)

39.   If a statement is a tautology its negation is a self-contradiction. Which of the following are self-contradictions?

(1) $-(S \equiv S)$?
(2) $S \equiv -S$?
(3) $(S \equiv T) \equiv (T \equiv S)$?
(4) $[S. (S \supset T)] \supset -T$?
(5) $S. -S$?

(Write the number or numbers, or "None")

---

(1), (2), (5)

END OF REVISION CHAPTER 2

Revision Chapter 3: Syllogisms and Quantifiers

This chapter is intended for the revision of the material of chapters 13 and 15 of the main part of the course.

1. In the diagram, points inside the left-hand circle, labelled "canaries", represent canaries; and points outside this circle, whether inside or outside the other 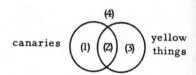 one, represent "non-canaries" -- that is, things other than canaries. Similarly, points inside the right-hand circle represent yellow things, points outside it non-yellow things.

There are four regions in the diagram, labelled respectively (1), (2), (3) and (4).
Region (1) represents non-yellow canaries.
What do the other regions, in order, represent?

---

(2) yellow canaries
(3) yellow non-canaries
(4) non-yellow non-canaries

2. We indicate that there is at least one thing in a given category by putting a stroke in the appropriate region. Thus in the diagram

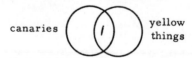

the stroke indicates that there is at least one yellow canary.

In the diagram

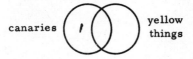

the stroke indicates that................

---

there is at least one non-yellow canary.

3. To indicate the <u>emptiness</u> of a given region we shade it out. In the diagram

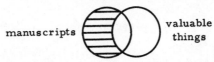

the shading indicates that there are no non-valuable manuscripts. In the diagram

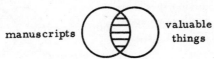

the shading indicates that ....

---

there are no valuable manuscripts.

4. A statement such as "There are no non-valuable manuscripts" can be expressed in the form "All manuscripts are valuable", provided we make a mental note that, in cases where the subject-term is empty, a statement of this form is to count as automatically true.

We adopt this convention in what follows. Hence "All As are Bs" is to be taken as meaning "There are no As that are not Bs". Shade the diagram to indicate this fact.

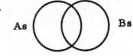

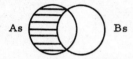

5.　Shade this diagram to represent the statement "No businessmen are trustworthy".

businessmen　trustworthy persons

---

businessmen　trustworthy persons

6.　Instead of "At least one A is a B" we shall write, for convenience, "Some A is a B" or "Some As are Bs", ignoring any subtle distinctions there may be between these formulations.
Mark this diagram to represent the statement "Some languages are easy to learn".

languages　things easy to learn

---

languages　things easy to learn

7.　Mark this diagram to represent both of the statements "Some locks are burglar-proof" and "Some locks are not burglar-proof".

locks　burglar-proof things

---

8.   What statement or statements does the following diagram represent?

(Say:)
"All hermits are misanthropes but not all misanthropes are hermits".

9.   In a diagram with three overlapping circles there are eight regions, and we shall sometimes want to mark regions in pairs.
In this diagram two adjoining regions are shaded. What single statement is represented?

"All brass things tarnish easily".

10.   We can use a three-circle diagram to demonstrate the validity of a syllogism; that is, of an argument such as the following.

(Premisses) { All mammals are warm-blooded
{ All domestic animals are mammals
(Conclusion) All domestic animals are warm-blooded

Here the first premiss is represented by horizontal shading and the second by vertical shading. The fact that the conclusion follows validly is indicated by the fact that the outlined region has been shaded in the process.

173

Mark the following diagram similarly to demonstrate the validity of the following syllogism.

(Premisses) { No hard-covers are cheap
{ All library-editions are hard-covers
(Conclusion) No library editions are cheap

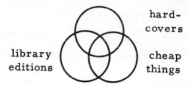

_____

Valid.

11. Where one premiss calls for shading and the other for a stroke, we should put the shading in first: this guarantees that the stroke may be put in <u>one</u> region only (since it need not run into the shaded region).

Draw a diagram for the following syllogism and say whether it is valid.

(Premisses) { All brass things tarnish easily
{ Some door-knockers are brass
(Conclusion) Some door-knockers tarnish easily

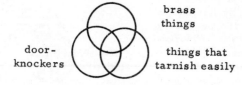

Valid.

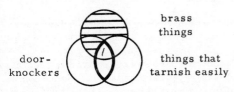

brass
things

door-
knockers

things that
tarnish easily

12. Draw a diagram for the following syllogism and say whether it is valid.

(Premisses) {All soccer fans are excitable
             {Some anglers are not excitable
(Conclusion) Some anglers are not soccer fans

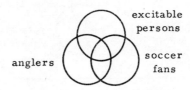

excitable
persons

anglers

soccer
fans

Valid.

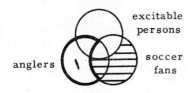

excitable
persons

anglers

soccer
fans

13. The following syllogism can be seen to be <u>invalid</u>:

(Premisses) {All tropical countries are
            {overpopulated
            {No tropical countries are
            {industrialised
(Conclusion) {No industrialised countries
             {are overpopulated.

175

Explain in your own words why the conclusion does not follow from the premisses.

(In suitable words:)
From the fact that all tropical countries are overpopulated it does not follow that <u>non</u>-tropical countries are <u>not</u> overpopulated. Hence there could be industrial countries which are n o n - t r o p i c a l but still over-populated.

14.   Draw a diagram for the inference in the previous example, outlining the region that should be shaded i f the conclusion were valid.

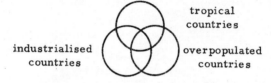

---

tropical
countries

industrialised
countries

overpopulated
countries

15.   A statement of the form "All As are Bs", represented on a diagram by shading, would normally be represented in modern logical symbols by using a <u>universal quantifier</u> and implication-sign, in the form

$$(x)(Ax \supset Bx).$$

This can be read "For all x, if x is an A, x is a B".
Write "All bachelors are happy" in this form, using "Bx" for "x is a bachelor" and "Hx" for "x is happy".

$(x)(Bx \supset Hx)$

16. "No As are Bs", which also involves shading, is the same as "All As are non-Bs" and is represented similarly, in the form
$$(x)(Ax \supset -Bx).$$
Write, using the same meanings as before, the statement "No bachelors are happy".

$(x)(Bx \supset -Hx)$

17. Many statements of more complicated form can be represented directly.
Write in symbols "Astrologers are either charlatans or simple-minded", using the letters "A", "C" and "S".

$(x)[Ax \supset (Cx \lor Sx)]$

18. A statement of the form "Some As are Bs", which we would represent on a diagram by means of a stroke, would normally be represented in symbols by means of an <u>existential quantifier</u> and conjunction; thus
$$(Ex)(Ax . Bx).$$
This might be read "For some x, x is an A and x is a B", where "some" is taken to mean "at least one" as before.
Write in symbols "Some reflexes are not conditioned", using "Rx" for "x is a reflex" and "Cx" for "x is conditioned".

$(Ex)(Rx. -Cx)$

19. "Some reflexes are not conditioned" can, however, be written in the form "It is not the case that all reflexes are conditioned"; that is, as the negation of a universal statement. Write the formula in this form.

$-(x)(Rx \supset Cx)$

20. In general we may write schematically
$$"(x)" \text{ is equivalent to } "-(Ex)-"$$

or conversely

"(Ex)" is equivalent to "-(x)-".

Hence (Ex)(Ax.-Bx) is equivalent to

$$-(x)\big[-(Ax.-Bx)\big].$$

(Note the bracketing.)

Show that -(Ax.-Bx) is equivalent to Ax ⊃ Bx by constructing a truth-table for -(p.-q) and comparing it with a table for p ⊃ q.

p	q	-q	p.-q	-(p.-q)	p ⊃ q
1	1				
1	0				
0	1				
0	0				

The last two columns both read "1 - 0 - 1 - 1".

21.   To what formula, with a universal quantifier and implication-sign, is -(Ex)(Ax.Bx) equivalent?

(x)(Ax ⊃ -Bx)

22.   This logical symbolism can be applied to inferences much more complicated than syllogisms are.   The rules for using it to test syllogisms are, however, very simple.   We first note that when we have two <u>universal</u> premisses we can roll them together into a single universal statement: thus the premisses

All Bs are Cs
All As are Bs

can be put as the conjunction

(x)(Bx ⊃ Cx) . (x)(Ax ⊃ Bx)

which is <u>equivalent to</u> the conjunction

(x)[(Bx ⊃ Cx) . (Ax ⊃ Bx)].

Write a similar expression for the pair of statements

No music-lovers are practical
All scientists are music-lovers

using "M", "P" and "S" for the predicates.

(x)[(Mx ⊃ -Px) . (Sx ⊃ Mx)]

23.   In the case of one universal premiss and one existential premiss we have a rule that the two <u>imply</u> an existential statement consisting of their conjunction. Thus

$$\text{All Bs are Cs}$$
$$\text{and Some As are Bs}$$

can be written together as

$$(x)(Bx \supset Cx).(Ex)(Ax.Bx)$$

which <u>implies</u>

$$(Ex)\left[(Bx \supset Cx).Ax.Bx\right].$$

Write a similar expression for a statement which is <u>implied by</u> the statements

$$\text{All virus diseases are contagious}$$
$$\text{Some skin diseases are not contagious}$$

using "V", "C" and "S" for the predicates.

$$(Ex)\left[(Vx \supset Cx).Sx.-Cx\right]$$

24.   Our third rule is that when any formula f_1 implies another formula f_2, the implication will remain valid if two similar quantifiers are put in front of them: that is

$$(x)(f_1) \text{ implies } (x)(f_2)$$
$$\text{and } (Ex)(f_1) \text{ implies } (Ex)(f_2).$$

By the "chain rule"

$$(Bx \supset Cx).(Ax \supset Bx) \text{ implies } Ax \supset Cx$$

and so, by the rule we have just stated

$$(x)\left[(Bx \supset Cx).(Ax \supset Bx)\right] \text{ implies } (x)(Ax \supset Cx).$$

State the premisses and conclusion of the syllogism this formula shows to be valid.

(Premisses) $\begin{cases} \text{All Bs are Cs} \\ \text{All As are Bs} \end{cases}$

(Conclusion) All As are Cs

25.   Similarly, the fact that

$$(Bx \supset Cx).Bx \text{ implies } Cx$$

so that

$$(Bx \supset Cx).Ax.Bx \text{ implies } Ax.Cx$$

leads, by the rule, to the fact that

$$(Ex)\left[(Bx \supset Cx).Ax.Bx\right]$$

implies

$$(Ex)(Ax.Cx).$$

179

The left-hand side is implied by
$$(x)(Bx \supset Cx) . (Ex)(Ax. Bx).$$
Hence state the premisses and conclusion of the syllogism we have shown to be valid.

(Premisses) $\begin{cases} \text{All Bs are Cs} \\ \text{Some As are Bs} \end{cases}$
(Conclusion) Some As are Cs

26. Show that the rules validate the syllogism

(Premisses) $\begin{cases} \text{All products of fermentation} \\ \text{contain alcohol} \\ \text{Nothing that contains alcohol} \\ \text{supports germs} \end{cases}$

(Conclusion) $\begin{cases} \text{Nothing that supports germs is} \\ \text{a product of fermentation} \end{cases}$

using "F", "A" and "G" for the predicates.

From
$(x)(Fx \supset Ax) . (x)(Ax \supset -Gx)$
we get
$(x)[(Fx \supset Ax). (Ax \supset -Gx)]$
which implies
$(x)(Fx \supset -Gx)$
equivalent by contraposition to
$(x)(Gx \supset -Fx).$

27. Show that the rules do not validate the invalid syllogism

(Premisses) $\begin{cases} \text{All virus diseases are contagious} \\ \text{Some pandemics are not virus diseases} \end{cases}$
(Conclusion) $\begin{cases} \text{Some pandemics are not contagious} \end{cases}$

using "V", "C" and "P" for the predicates.

From
$(x)(Vx \supset Cx).(Ex)(Px.-Vx)$
we get
$(Ex)[(Vx \supset Cx).Px.-Vx]$
but from
$(Vx \supset Cx) . -Vx$
we cannot deduce $-Cx$, and so this does <u>not</u> imply $(Ex)(Px.-Cx)$.

    28.   Write the statement
               No European alphabets are pictorial
in symbols, using "U" (for "is European "), "A" and "P" for the
other predicates.

$(x)[(Ux.Ax) \supset -Px]$

    29.   The inference

                           No European alphabets are
(Premisses)   pictorial
                           All alphabets are either
                           pictorial or phonetic
                           All European alphabets are
(Conclusion)   phonetic

is not a syllogism in the strict sense of the word, since it contains
four distinct terms and each statement contains three of them.
Show, however, that it can be validated by the rules. (Use "H" for
"is phonetic".)

$(x)[(Ux.Ax) \supset -Px].(x)[Ax \supset (Px \vee Hx)]$
is equivalent to
$(x)\{[(Ux.Ax) \supset -Px].[Ax \supset (Px \vee Hx)]\}$
Now if Ux.Ax implies $-Px$ and also $Px \vee Hx$ it must imply Hx.
Hence we have
$(x)[(Ux.Ax) \supset Hx]$.

<u>END OF REVISION CHAPTER 3</u>

Appendix to Chapter 12

Table of possible relations between two statements.

p true, q true	p true, q false	p false, q true	p false, q false	Relation of p to q.
possible	possible	possible	possible	Indifference
impossible	possible	possible	possible	Contrariety
possible	impossible	possible	possible	Superimplication.
impossible	impossible	possible	possible	p impossible, q contingent
possible	possible	impossible	possible	Subimplication.
impossible	possible	impossible	possible	q impossible, p contingent
possible	impossible	impossible	possible	Equivalence
impossible	impossible	impossible	possible	p impossible, q impossible
possible	possible	possible	impossible	Subcontrariety
impossible	possible	possible	impossible	Contradiction.
possible	impossible	possible	impossible	q tautology, p contingent
impossible	impossible	possible	impossible	p impossible, q tautology
possible	possible	impossible	impossible	p tautology, q contingent
impossible	possible	impossible	impossible	p tautology, q impossible
possible	impossible	impossible	impossible	p tautology, q tautology